"*Facilitating Counseling Groups* is a comprehensive guide for churches who want to train lay leaders on how to facilitate group-based counseling ministry using the G4 model, which emphasizes targeted discipleship. I highly recommend this excellent resource to all church leaders who want to bring healing and hope to those in their congregation who are hurting and need more support. This is the best-kept secret that the church needs today."

Shannon Kay McCoy, Biblical Counseling Director, Valley Center Community Church; council member, Biblical Counseling Coalition; author of *Help! I'm A Slave to Food*

"For those who have no experience with group counseling, this book is highly accessible. For those looking to enhance their existing groups ministry, this book is remarkably comprehensive. As more biblical counselors embrace the validity of groups, this book will surely become THE guide for facilitating from a biblical perspective."

David and Krista Dunham, Counselors, Sparrow & Heart Soul Care; authors of *Table for Two: Biblical Counsel for Eating Disorders*

"*Facilitating Counseling Groups* is one of the rare how-to books that answers more questions than it raises. You'll discover how a group's needs reveal the best way to help its members, how to deal with challenging participants and circumstances, what your goals should be for each stage of your group, and more. *Facilitating* finally takes the mystery out of leading counseling groups."

Sam Hodges IV, President, Church Initiative (GriefShare and DivorceCare)

"Almost fifteen years ago I started biblical counseling in a group format. It is one of the most impactful things a church can do to build a soul-care culture. Brad and John have laid out a helpful step-by-step approach to getting group-based discipleship and care going in your church. This book is long overdue, and I recommend it to anyone considering building a recovery or soul-care ministry that includes a group format."

Garrett Higbee, President, Soul Care Consulting; director, Lead Healthy Retreats (TSNI)

"I'm often asked, 'How can I get equipped for ministry?' *Facilitating Counseling Groups* is one of the best group-based ministry-equipping tools I've ever read! It provides detailed, practical guidance from two leaders who have been equipped personally through years in the trenches of face-to-face ministry with sufferers and sinners. This book gives you priceless wisdom for your ministry tool belt."

Ellen Mary Dykas, Director of Equipping for Ministry to Women, Harvest USA; author of *Jesus and Your Unwanted Journey: Wives Finding Comfort after Sexual Betrayal*

FACILITATING COUNSELING GROUPS

FACILITATING COUNSELING GROUPS

A LEADER'S GUIDE FOR CHURCH-BASED COUNSELING MINISTRY

Brad Hambrick and John Chapman

New Growth Press, Greensboro, NC 27401

Cover Design: Faceout Books, faceoutstudio.com
Interior Typesetting and eBook: Lisa Parnell, lparnellbookservices.com

ISBN: 978-1-64507-331-4 (Print)
ISBN: 978-1-64507-332-1 (eBook)

Library of Congress Cataloging-in-Publication Data on file

Printed in the United States of America

30 29 28 27 26 25 24 23 1 2 3 4 5

CONTENTS

FOREWORD

Around The Summit Church, we have a handful of sayings we call "plumb lines"—short, pithy statements that help us direct and measure our ministry. Brick masons use plumb lines to build a wall straight and true. Our plumb lines help us build God's church the same way.

One of my favorite Summit plumb lines is this: "Show your work and let others copy your paper." No, this isn't a plumb line endorsing plagiarism. It captures our desire to do our ministry work with intentionally open hands. What we do in *our* church, for *our* people, in *our* context—and this local context is always paramount—just might be fruitful for other churches and people and contexts.

Multiplication is at the heart of the Great Commission. We are not only supposed to do our work well, but to teach others to do it also—sometimes better than we do it. We are called not only to be successful, but to reproduce. If God prospers you at something, take that extra time to write down the secrets of your success so that others can do it too. Though that might feel at times like a cumbersome process, the benefit it brings to others will more than make up for any inconvenience. Proverbs 12:27 (NIV) says, "The lazy do not roast any game, but the diligent feed on the riches of the hunt." "Making the kill" is only half the success of hunting; dress the game and get it into the refrigerator so that others can feast on your success later!

When I think of people who do this well, at the top of the list is our pastor of counseling, Brad Hambrick. I know few people with the wisdom and insight he possesses. But Brad is also a master at showing his work. Which is precisely what he does here, in *Mobilizing Church-Based Counseling* and *Facilitating Counseling Groups*. He's showing his work, letting your church replicate two highly effective, much-needed ministries.

G4 (support and recovery groups) and Gospel-Centered Marriage (our premarital counseling ministry) are two ministries that have mobilized our members and served the Summit well for over a decade. I cannot imagine the life of The Summit Church without them. Or, maybe more honestly, I don't want to.

I've seen more lives changed as a result of these ministries than I can recount. But it's not the result of Brad's magical hand. It's the result of a gospel-driven process—one that your church can and should learn.

We end every worship service at the Summit with a simple commission: "You are sent." It's a reminder that every member of our church has been sent by God to bring God's healing and hope into the world.

That's my dream for these books, too. We are sending them out into the world to bring God's healing and hope—beginning, perhaps today, with your church.

J. D. Greear
Lead Pastor, The Summit Church, Raleigh-Durham, NC

A Word to the Reader:

DON'T SKIP THIS

As you begin reading this book, you and your church are in one of two places:

1. Your church has already initiated a G4 ministry and you are preparing to be a new leader within an existing G4 ministry.
2. You have worked through *Mobilizing Church-Based Counseling* with your church leadership and are now preparing to launch the first G4 group at your church.

If you're thinking, *Wait! I'm number three—I'm not at a church with an established G4 ministry, and I have not read* Mobilizing, then *Facilitating* (this book) should probably be the second book you read. Metaphorically, *Mobilizing* helps you and your church build the airport for the plane (i.e., ministry), while *Facilitating* teaches you to fly. Regardless, thank you for embarking on this journey and allowing your story to be a conduit of God's care to people on a comparable journey.

If your church has an established G4 ministry, you've heard about G4 for a while, have probably been to an evening of group meetings, and have had the opportunity to talk to other G4 leaders. This familiarity with G4 will serve you well as you seek to assimilate the material in the pages ahead.

But if you are between *Mobilizing* and *Facilitating*—that is, between "building the airport" and "flying" your church's first G4 group—don't worry. By the time you reach the culmination of this book in chapter 23 and review your job description as a G4 facilitator, you will have become an expert on G4. You will be ready to answer questions from new group participants who come with the same uncertainty and questions you have right now.

You'll notice that we put your job description as the final chapter of this book. We want to use it as a review-and-encouragement tool. By the time you arrive at your job description, we want it to feel as familiar and comfortable as an old pair of house slippers. If you're wired differently and want to see the role laid out first, feel free to skip to the end, read chapter 23, and then begin reading chapter 1.

The chapters in the introductory section (chapters 1–5) will give you an overview of G4, which is a group-based counseling ministry designed to be led by laypeople in a local church context. This book and your group curriculum serve as the only training you'll need to be a G4 facilitator. As you read, you'll learn to appreciate why we call G4 leaders "facilitators." You can use the terms *G4 leaders* and *facilitators* interchangeably.

After we help you differentiate G4 from other ministries in your church and understand G4's core values, we'll prepare you for your role in three sections. The sections are successive, with each laying the foundation for the next.

- We'll walk you through **a night at G4**. This will orient you to G4's "order of service." In section one (chapters 6–11), you'll learn *what* happens *when*.
- We'll walk you through the **growth journey of a G4 participant**. This is why G4 exists. You want to see lives change. In section two (chapters 12–16), you'll learn the role of curriculum at G4.
- We'll walk you through **the stages of a group as a collective organism**. In section three (chapters 17–23), you'll learn the

difference between being the counselor for ten individuals sitting in a circle (not your role) and being the person who cares for the group as people walk their individual journeys of change.

The good news is you don't have to know what any of that means yet. You'll learn that in the pages ahead. If you understand the outline, you're ready to get started.

An Introduction to G4

Chapter 1

THANK YOU FOR EMBODYING 2 CORINTHIANS 1:3–5

A theme passage for G4 and church-based counseling groups is 2 Corinthians 1:3–5:

> Blessed be the God and Father of our Lord Jesus Christ, the Father of mercies and *God of all comfort, who comforts us in all our affliction, so that we may be able to comfort those who are in any affliction, with the comfort with which we ourselves are comforted by God*. For as we share abundantly in Christ's sufferings, so through Christ we share abundantly in comfort too. (emphasis added)

You have been through some hard things. God has been faithful. You are in a better place. Now you want to allow the story of God's faithfulness in your life to be part of facilitating change in the lives of others. That's awesome! Thank you!

To ask the cliché counseling question: how does that make you feel? Excited? Nervous? Eager to get started? Unsure where to begin? Intimidated by possibilities? Willing to trust God with the uncertainty?

These are normal responses as you consider taking on a leadership role within a ministry like G4. The absence of these up-and-down, excited-yet-nervous emotions would reveal more of a problem—either pride or indifference—than their presence, which indicates humility and expectancy. This leads to the natural questions, *Am I ready? Is it wise for me to step into this role at this time?* For help answering these questions, consider the following two things:

- First, identify any red flags. Red flags are *secrets and recent setbacks*. A primary task of a G4 leader is modeling honesty. Group-based counseling ministries are famous for saying, "You're only as healthy as your secrets." If there's a major element of your struggle you haven't confided to anyone yet, hold off on leading. Or if you've faced a significant setback in your struggle recently, it's better to participate in a group, support the current leader, and continue to work toward being a future leader.
- Second, pay attention to your response as you read *Facilitating*. Chapter by chapter, you'll ask yourself, *Do I get excited about this?* The more times you answer yes, the better fit G4 is for you. This book is a guided tour of what being a G4 leader entails. If reading this book doesn't excite you, God probably has another ministry for you. That's great too!

At this stage in your journey, you don't need to decide anything. You just need to be honest about how you respond to the pages ahead. Trust God to make it clear whether leadership in G4 is a good fit for you. If your church has an established G4 ministry, allow those who are already leading to speak into the decision as they share what being a G4 leader has been like for them.

Read this book with the same faith and vulnerability that every participant will be asked to begin their G4 journey with. At the beginning of any journey, we don't know the outcome. We begin by trusting God to faithfully provide what we need as we engage the next step in the process.

Chapter 2

INTRODUCING THE THREE LIFE CYCLES OF GROUPS-BASED COUNSELING

When you read the section headings in the table of contents, you may have wondered, *What are the three life cycles of a church-based groups ministry?* You began to get a sense for what these life cycles were when reading the introduction. Now we'll introduce each life cycle more extensively.

You might be asking what *life cycle* means. We are using the term *life cycle* as a metaphor for parts of the G4 experience that have their own beginning (birth), middle (growth/development), and end (resolution). As a prospective leader, it is helpful to have each life cycle in mind because the leader's role is to nurture each life cycle's growth and development as they facilitate their group.

1. **A night of G4** is designed so that everything from the parking lot to the closing debrief helps to facilitate growth in participants and reinforce ministry culture.
2. Individual **group members** grow in ways we also call a life cycle. The curriculum for each group outlines this journey for that subject.
3. **The group itself** has an independent life cycle that is easy to overlook; hence, you as the group leader will need to nurture the group through its stages of growth and maturity.

As a G4 leader, we want you to understand each life cycle so you can reinforce the benefits and navigate the challenges inherent to each life cycle.

What we begin in this chapter, we will complete in the three major sections of this book. This chapter is merely the initial orientation. Here we will overview the map. In the pages that follow, we will explore the terrain of each life cycle. If you understand the big picture after this chapter, you'll be ready for the remainder of the book.

LIFE CYCLE ONE: AN EVENING OF G4 MINISTRY

We cover this life cycle first to give you the mental scaffolding for what happens at G4. As you get to know the flow and schedule of G4, it will help you locate when and where the things we discuss in the next two life cycles actually happen.

If your church only has one or two G4 groups, this life cycle will be truncated. You will welcome new guests and conduct your subject-specific group. But once you have a collection of G4 groups meeting at the same time and location, you will have a G4 director[1] who leads a large group time and a debrief to care for G4 leaders.

There are two primary goals in this life cycle. First, these weekly rhythms establish a consistent culture between the various G4 groups, helping participants understand what they should expect from their G4 experience. Second, these weekly rhythms ensure that there is a culture of care among G4 leaders to help them not just persevere, but thrive, amid an emotionally weighty ministry.

In chapters 7–10, we will discuss the following four components of a night of G4:

- Welcome: From the Parking Lot to "Hello" (chapter 7)
- Large Group: Reinforcing the Culture of G4 (chapter 8)

1. *Mobilizing Church-Based Counseling* is the training manual for your G4 director in the same way that this book is the training manual for G4 leaders.

- Subject-Specific Groups: Working on Life Struggles (chapter 9)
- Debrief: Caring for Your G4 Leaders (chapter 10)

As a G4 leader, you are primarily responsible for your subject-specific group (chapter 9). But you may also have a role in the welcome time or large group time. Your G4 director bears the responsibility for coordinating details related to welcome, large group, and debrief times.

Your goal in studying the full life cycle (even the parts that aren't your primary responsibility) is twofold. First, *learn how to encourage, appreciate, and assist your G4 director*. They need support and encouragement in their role, just like you do in your role. Understanding and valuing their role well enough to cooperate with it encourages your director in the way that group participants coming fully prepared for an evening encourages you.

Second, *you want to understand the function of each part of an evening of G4 so that you can ensure everyone present (including you) experiences the intended effect*. Understanding the intended function of each part of an evening at G4 prevents us from mindlessly going through the motions.

LIFE CYCLE TWO: THE JOURNEY OF EACH PARTICIPANT

The personal journey of each participant is in the second life cycle. This life cycle is the most foundational for G4. Every G4 participant comes with a goal: to overcome a struggle, to process an experience, to find support for a journey, or to understand a challenge. This work constitutes the primary life cycle of G4. The other two life cycles exist to assist this one.

Each curriculum in the G4 series is built around one of two nine-step models: one for sin-based struggles or one for suffering-based struggles (see appendix A for a list of G4 curriculums). We will give an overview of these two models in chapters 13 and 14.[2]

2. We will discuss how to utilize non-nine-step curriculums in chapter 15.

The rationale for having two distinct nine-step models is to represent the reality that the gospel speaks to sin and suffering in different ways: *offering forgiveness and freedom from sin and providing comfort and meaning amid suffering*. As people, we are simultaneously sinner and sufferer, so we need both forgiveness and comfort. But with each life struggle, sin or suffering is usually more in the foreground.[3]

As a G4 leader, you will be helping participants navigate the steps in their journeys. This involves providing a safe place for them to talk about their struggle, facilitating application-based discussions of the group curriculum, modeling honesty and perspective about your own journey, and normalizing the common challenges related to the subject of your group. As we'll say many times, G4 leaders are not "counseling experts"; instead, they are caring lay leaders who have experience walking a shared journey.

Most G4 groups follow an open group model. This means that each participant works at their own pace. In chapter 17 we'll provide guidance on how to lead an open group where each participant is at a different point in their journey. For now, you need to know that you are *not* responsible to try to synchronize the progress of the participants in your group.

As a G4 leader, your role is to be aware of where each participant is in their journey. *However, you are not a counselor for each participant in the group. You are the facilitator of the group as a whole.* That is why we begin from this point forward using the term *G4 facilitator* to describe your role—rather than *G4 leader*—although it is fine to use these titles interchangeably.

This leads us to our third life cycle: the life of the group.

LIFE CYCLE THREE: THE COLLECTIVE LIFE OF THE GROUP

Think of the group as its own organism. The group will go through stages of development, but the life of the group will not be as linear

3. An excellent follow-up to this book would be Michael Emlet's *Saints, Sufferers, and Sinners: Loving Others as God Loves Us*, Helping the Helper series (Greensboro, NC: New Growth Press, 2021).

as this outline. When new people enter the group and existing members graduate from it, the culture of group will move forward and backward, like the ocean tide, through the five stages. Each of these stages is described in its own chapter.

- Stage One: Creating a Sense of "Us" (chapter 18)
- Stage Two: Navigating Resistance to Change (chapter 19)
- Stage Three: Creating a Shared Culture (chapter 20)
- Stage Four: Doing the Hard Work of Change (chapter 21)
- Stage Five: Graduating and Celebrating Friends (chapter 22)

Your responsibility is to keep an eye on where the group is within these stages and work to alleviate the challenges that come with each stage. The social dynamics of a group have great power to either promote or hinder change. Your role as a G4 facilitator is to harness this power for a positive effect. Sometimes that is as simple as naming a challenge so that the group feels free to talk about it. We'll discuss these challenges in section three.

WHERE DO WE GO FROM HERE?

We will devote a full section of this book to each of these three life cycles. But before we do that, we will do three more things. First, we will help you understand how G4 differs from the general discipleship groups in your church (chapter 3). Second, we will define the seven core values of G4 so you know the DNA you are seeking to infuse through each life cycle (chapter 4). Third, we will give you a list of key G4 roles and terms (chapter 5).

Chapter 3

HOW G4 GROUPS DIFFER FROM YOUR CHURCH'S SMALL GROUPS

When anyone in your church or community asks, "What is G4?" or "What would I get from a G4 group?" you want everyone to receive a consistent answer. Whether you're leading a group on addiction, eating disorders, purity, trauma, or another life struggle, we want you to communicate shared DNA that is the essence of a G4 ministry.

Read this chapter slowly. After each section, pause and restate the content in your own words. You will be ready to move to chapter 4 when you can conversationally explain what you've read in this chapter to someone who has never attended G4.

WHAT IS G4?

G4 is a lay-led, group-based counseling ministry built around two nine-step models of change. G4 provides a context for participants to invest a season of their life overcoming a life-dominating struggle of sin or suffering. With the support of their fellow group members, G4 participants work through a biblically based curriculum focused on their primary life struggle.

The goal of G4 is to see participants graduate back into the discipleship ministries of their church, freer from their struggle and with a clearer picture of what it means for believers to care for one another as the gospel transforms the most difficult parts of our lives.

WHY THE NAME "G4"?

"G" is for **g**ospel-centered **g**roups. Too often in counseling groups our struggle becomes our identity. The longer someone is in group, the more their identity becomes "addict," "depressed," or "divorced." The benefit of finding a place to be known comes with the potential drawback of embracing a struggle-based identity.

We place the "G" at the forefront of G4 to serve as a perpetual reminder that our identity is not found in our struggle but in our Savior—Jesus Christ. Yes, we struggle. Yes, it is freeing to have a place to be honest about our struggle. But, no, our struggle does not define us. The gospel tells us who we are and has the power to transform us into the person God created us to be.

The number **"4"** is for the **four** classifications of groups that can be housed within a G4 ministry. Not all counseling groups are the same. If you put one type of group at the forefront of your ministry, it inadvertently communicates a limited scope of care. For instance, if you label your ministry a *recovery ministry*, it gives the impression that it only deals with addiction. We chose the name G4 to prevent it from being unduly associated with only one niche of life struggles. A basic definition for each of the four types of groups follows:

1. *Recovery Groups* are for overcoming destructive, habituated life patterns a participant wants to remove from their life. Recovery groups are for struggles like substance abuse, chemical addiction, or behavioral addictions (i.e., pornography or gambling).
2. *Process Groups* are for decreasing the life disruption caused by profoundly difficult experiences or especially "sticky" emotions. Process groups are for experiences such as trauma or the aftermath of destructive relationships.

3. *Support Groups* are for mutual encouragement as participants persevere through difficult life experiences that persist for an indefinite length of time. Support groups are for experiences like divorce, depression, or grief.
4. *Therapeutic Educational Groups* provide a better understanding of life challenges that are commonly misunderstood. Therapeutic educational groups might offer a holistic Christian perspective on mental health or help participants identify common challenges for blended families.

A G4 ministry does not need to have a group from each type to be called G4. For instance, if a church only had recovery groups and process groups in its offerings, it would *not* be called G2. Further, the types of groups are not as distinct as they initially appear. All groups, to some degree, offer therapeutic education. Every type of group involves processing difficult experiences together. It is not important that every group fit neatly into one of the four types. It is important to be clear what distinguishes G4 groups from general discipleship groups or classes within your church.

The goal of a benign name like G4 is to destigmatize a ministry that might otherwise be hard to talk about. Participants can say "I've got a G4 meeting tonight" without disclosing more than they intend. A pastor preaching on purity can talk about the G4 groups at church without trying to define sexual addiction. A ministry that depends on word of mouth needs to be easy to talk about.

G4 was also designed to house non-nine-step groups. We intentionally created G4 to allow you to use more than just G4 nine-step curriculums. We will talk about that in chapter 15.

WHAT ARE DIFFERENCES BETWEEN A SMALL GROUP AND A G4 GROUP?

Now that you understand the various purposes G4 groups can serve, we can begin to differentiate G4 from the general discipleship groups in your church, whether your church calls those Sunday school classes, life groups, community groups, small groups, or something else. We can begin identifying important distinctions by asking, "What does a general small group look like?" While the structure can vary from church to church, most general discipleship groups have some common features. A small group usually consists of seven to fifteen people who meet weekly to discuss the Bible, pray, care for one another, and do ministry together.

The following description can help you understand what makes G4 different:

- G4 groups meet for a *narrow purpose*, to address a specific struggle or life transition.
- G4 groups are a place to overcome a struggle rather than "do ministry together."
- G4 is not a Bible study. It is a counseling group that utilizes a distinctively Christian curriculum to help participants grow in a particular area of their life.
- G4 groups are short-term and are not intended to be a participant's ongoing source of community.

Small groups focus on *general discipleship*—cultivating the overall spiritual maturity of believers who are facing a variety of life challenges—while G4 does *targeted discipleship*—setting aside a season of life to overcome a specific struggle with people facing a similar struggle.

General discipleship groups are often organized around factors like age (i.e., young adults, seniors, etc.), geography (i.e., driving distance to a host home), or relational status (i.e., young couples or singles). G4 groups organize around a common life struggle.

No one graduates from a general discipleship group. There's always more character refinement to be done and more to understand in the Bible. In G4, participants remain in their group only until they reach a satisfying level of change for their life struggle.

G4 and general discipleship groups should have a symbiotic relationship, each giving life to the other. G4 provides a space for people to focus on a single area of needed change. This prevents general discipleship groups from being overwhelmed by an intense need in the life of one member. General discipleship groups provide a context of support after G4, so that G4 doesn't inadvertently reinforce a struggle-based identity.

CHAPTER 3 FINAL EXAM

Recall the questions with which we began this chapter. Imagine a fellow church member asking you what G4 is and how it's different from other small groups. If you feel conversationally comfortable answering these questions, you are ready to proceed to chapter 4.

Chapter 4

SEVEN CORE VALUES OF G4

Now we'll delve deeper into the DNA of G4, the values at the heart of the ministry. The last two chapters have been about how you *define* and *explain* G4. This chapter is about what you *embody* through G4.

G4 has seven core values. When you ask yourself *How am I doing as a G4 leader?* these seven values provide your performance review checklist. If you are considering a new curriculum, these values serve as the matrix for evaluating it. As a prospective leader in G4, you are asking, *Do these values represent who I want to be and what I want to do?*

VALUE ONE: G4 IS BIBLE-BASED AND GOSPEL-CENTERED

Programs like G4 do not change people. The Holy Spirit brings about heart level change. This means that information and insight alone are not adequate for lasting change. Instead, it is ultimately the power of the gospel that enables people to find hope and enact change. We believe that the power of the gospel is communicated best through a combination of words and relationships. Therefore, both the group experience (i.e., relationships) and biblically based curriculum (i.e., words) are vital aspects of G4.

Scripture is central to G4. The Bible is our ultimate source of hope and meaning. G4 curriculums strive to utilize the Bible responsibly, with sound hermeneutics (i.e., principles of interpretation), and within a healthy theology of emotions and relationships. Our desire is for G4 groups to have honest, biblically based conversations about areas of our life that need to change.

VALUE TWO: G4 RECOGNIZES THE DIFFERENCE BETWEEN SIN AND SUFFERING

While both sin and suffering have a common origin in the Genesis 3 fall, there are differences in how we experience them and how we find freedom from their effects. At G4, we believe that the Bible speaks to both sin and suffering but offers different solutions to each. That's why we have two nine-step models. *The gospel offers forgiveness and freedom from sin, and comfort and meaning amid suffering*. Yet neither sin nor suffering will be completely remedied until we arrive in heaven.

It is not that some people are sinners and other people are sufferers. As Christians, we are all simultaneously saint, sinner, and sufferer. However, particular struggles are rooted more (not entirely) in either sin or suffering. Some struggles emerge from our unbiblical beliefs, values, and choices. Other struggles emerge from living in a broken world, among fellow sinners, and with bodies affected by the fall. This is why each G4 group utilizes either a responsibility-based (sin) or suffering-focused model.

VALUE THREE: G4 IS BUILT ON HONESTY AND TRANSPARENCY

Outside of the Bible, the most powerful tool for change is honesty. Unless we are honest with God, ourselves, and others we squelch the power of the Bible to transform our lives. This is why a G4 plumb line is, "You will never be more free than you are honest." G4 groups are meant to create a space for open and honest conversations about our struggles and hardships.

Because honesty is so powerful, it is critical that G4 groups foster an environment where it is safe to be transparent. As new participants enter G4, honesty may not be their native language. The honesty of the G4 leader and members should serve as an example to emulate—one that is attractive because of its authenticity and liberating effect. G4 may be the first place some of us feel safe being fully known, an experience we begin desiring to permeate more and more spheres of our life.

VALUE FOUR: G4 UPHOLDS CONFIDENTIALITY

To steward the core value of honesty and transparency, G4 must uphold the core value of confidentiality. In G4 groups, participants mutually steward the honor and responsibility of knowing each other's stories. The shared code within G4 is "You decide who knows your story. When you decide to share your story *with* our group, you are not agreeing to share your story *through* us to anyone else."[1]

To uphold the value of honesty and transparency requires *courage* on the part of the person who is sharing. To uphold the value of confidentiality requires *integrity* from the other members of the group. These two values are more intertwined than any other set of values on this list. Honoring the value of confidentiality is one of the most effective ways to invite honesty from other group members.

VALUE FIVE: G4 AVOIDS STRUGGLE-BASED IDENTITY

The longer we struggle with a particular sin or form of suffering, the more that struggle begins to define us. Our identity mutates from being a person who struggles with addiction, depression, or the effects of divorce to being an addict, depressed, or divorced. When this happens, we face two challenges: (a) the struggle itself and (b) an identity increasingly rooted in that struggle. At G4, our desire is to more fully embrace the identity that we have been freely given through the acceptance of Jesus Christ as a central part of finding freedom from our struggles.

Therefore, at G4, we are careful about the identity language we use. We neither minimize our struggles nor define ourselves

---

1. The exception to this principle is the same that exists in any counseling setting: instances of mandated reporting emerging from the abuse/neglect of a minor and the endangerment of self or others. For guidance on how to respond to these situations see www.churchcares.com.

by our struggles. Groups may be defined by a particular struggle because of the shared experience that brings us together, but individuals have names, not labels. When you come to G4, we want you to know there will be people who greet you with a smile, make eye contact, and call you by name. Your struggle is not who you are; it is only part of your story we are working together to overcome.

VALUE SIX: G4 BLENDS DISCIPLESHIP, ACCOUNTABILITY, AND A GUIDED PROCESS

G4 is more (not less) than a practical Bible study on a particular topic. The goal of G4 is not primarily education, but transformation, and it draws upon three elements to facilitate this transformation.

Discipleship: The depth and duration of change we experience is highly correlated with the life rhythms that reinforce that change. G4 draws upon the discipleship rhythms of the Christian life—Bible study (cognitive change), discussion (social reinforcement), and disclosure/confession (personal sacrifice)—to facilitate a model of change that will be reinforced for as long as the participant remains meaningfully engaged in a local church.

Accountability: Accountability should be expressed not only in a set of questions asked weekly but also in a mutual embrace of a shared goal and objective (i.e., the subject matter of the group). Accountability should focus as much on the positive (what we're pursuing) as the negative (what we're removing). G4 is a place where we mutually reinforce the pursuit of a God-honoring, personally satisfying life where our struggle is consistently less present.

A Guided Process: G4 curriculums provide more of a map for a journey than an outline of a subject. In other words, the G4 curriculum focuses more on the process of growth and change than on the acquisition of knowledge. A participant's readiness to move forward in the curriculum is determined by their having reached certain growth markers, not by their having understood certain content. At G4, our curriculum keeps us on task working toward change and prevents us from getting lost in discussing ideas and sharing stories.

VALUE SEVEN: G4 TRANSITIONS INTO THE CHURCH'S DISCIPLESHIP MINISTRIES

G4 is a temporary place of safety, rest, and restoration. Participants do not permanently attend G4, but instead graduate into the general discipleship ministries of the church. A focused time of overcoming a life-dominating struggle of sin or suffering is good. But a groups ministry that does not graduate participants inadvertently reinforces a struggle-based identity and can create a church within a church.

A church's general discipleship ministries benefit from an infusion of G4 graduates. These graduates model higher levels of honesty and transparency that elevate the discipleship temperature in the entire church. And G4 needs the church so that overcoming a struggle doesn't get portrayed as the ultimate goal of life. We overcome struggles to free more of our life to live on mission for God. Embedding G4 in the church and graduating participants into the church protects the balance of these values.

CONCLUSION

This chapter has explained the essence of G4—its heartbeat. The difference between this chapter and the chapters that follow is kind of like the contrast between naming a superhero's special power and defining the essence of being a hero. Superman can fly. The Hulk is crazy strong. Flash is phenomenally fast. This is what each hero "does," but it is not what a hero "is." A hero is marked by a set of qualities: courage, loyalty, perseverance, and, perhaps most importantly, honor. Without these qualities, someone possessing special powers is a villain to be feared, not a hero to be admired.

This chapter hasn't been about defining what a G4 group "does." That's what the rest of this book is about. This chapter has been about defining the seven core values of what a G4 group "is." On your journey toward becoming a G4 leader, the question you need to be asking yourself is, *Do these values reflect the kind of person I want to be and the kind of ministry I want to lead?* If the answer is yes, let's continue.

Chapter 5

LEARNING G4 ROLES AND TERMS

This chapter will feel a bit different because it is staccato and doesn't flow. But it is also important. Every ministry develops some of its own language. The more niche a ministry is, the more unique its terms. The narrow focus of G4 means there are some words and phrases you'll need to learn.

You may want to dog-ear this page so can find this chapter quickly as you read. Throughout *Facilitating* you will come across terms and think, *I want to make sure I understand this word as it's being used.* That is an indication you need to flip back to chapter 5. In time, these terms will become intuitive to you, but in the early stages of orienting yourself to your new role, this chapter helps you avoid feeling like your fellow G4 leaders are speaking a foreign language.

Most of these terms you've already heard us use. Here you'll find them laid out in a way that makes it easier to find each term. This chapter is laid out in four sections, with terms in each section introduced either ordinally (as they occur in the life of a G4 ministry) or according to prioritization. The four sections include:

1. Training materials for G4
2. Roles and people in G4
3. G4 gathering types
4. Other G4 lingo

TRAINING MATERIALS FOR G4

- **Mobilizing**—the one-word reference to the book *Mobilizing Church-Based Counseling: Models for Sustainable Church-Based Care*, which was written for the person overseeing this ministry (G4 director), church leadership, and G4 facilitators who are beginning to mentor a coleader. *Mobilizing* delves into how the G4 counseling model fits into the wider world of counseling, and it gives step-by-step guidance on launching a new G4 ministry. It also introduces a model for mentored premarital counseling called *Creating a Gospel-Centered Marriage* (GCM).
- **Facilitating**—the one-word reference for this book, *Facilitating Church-Based Counseling Groups*, written for new leaders and coleaders learning the role of being a G4 facilitator. It is the resource G4 directors use to orient new group leaders to G4.
- **Curriculum**—The written and/or video content around which G4 leaders facilitate discussion for their subject-specific group. G4's nine-step curriculum and how to find them are listed in appendix A. In addition to *Facilitating*, you will need to select a curriculum and familiarize yourself with it before launching a group.

ROLES AND PEOPLE IN G4

- **G4 director**—The individual responsible for the weekly operation and oversight of G4 at your church. They vet and train new leaders, oversee the care of existing G4 leaders, and serve as the liaison between G4 and the pastoral staff. At most churches, this is a volunteer position.
- **G4 facilitators (a.k.a., G4 leaders or group leaders)**—This is the role you are preparing for, serving as a G4 group leader. Their training involves having personal life experience with the subject of the group (addiction, eating disorder, trauma, etc.), completing the *Facilitating* training, and studying their group's curriculum.

- **Church leadership**—Refers to the pastors, elders, and other designated leaders of your church (may vary based upon your church's polity). Once you have enough G4 groups to have a G4 director, you will report to your G4 director, who will report to a designated member of your church's leadership team.
- **Community partners**—Professionals in your community who provide counseling-related services. G4 may refer to these people when a participant has needs that exceed G4's capacity to care, and these people may refer their clients to G4 when peer support is a good supplement to their work. Community partners also include non-counselors in your community who refer to G4.
- **Counseling consultant**—A professional counselor in your community who consults with your G4 director (see appendix B) when difficult situations emerge in your ministry. You as a facilitator bring the situation to your G4 director, and your director will get guidance from the counseling consultant to assist you in leading your group and caring for this individual.
- **First-time guest**—The preferred way to reference people that many churches refer to as *visitors*. Saying "We have a *visitor* with us tonight" inadvertently implies you don't expect them to be around long. Saying "We have a *guest* with us tonight" conveys more honor and excitement about their presence.[1]
- **Group member**—Someone is considered a *member* of a G4 group when they commit to the group and to completing their curriculum journey. In an open group model, the distinction between guests and members is important in order

---

1. For more guidance on creating a welcoming presence throughout your church for first-time guests, we recommend Danny Franks's book *People Are the Mission: How Churches Can Welcome Guests Without Compromising the Gospel* (Grand Rapids, MI: Zondervan, 2018).

to highlight the significance of commitment for G4 to be effective.

- **Group participant**—A reference to everyone present, both guests and members. The reference is often shortened to *participants* while talking to group members.
- **Support network**—These are the positive influences in a participant's life outside of G4. These people may include family, friends, or other counselors. These are the individuals to whom the baton of support, accountability, and encouragement will be passed when this person graduates from G4.

G4 GATHERING TYPES

- **Large group**—The early part of an evening at G4 when participants from all the subject-specific groups gather briefly in one room. This time allows the G4 leadership team to teach the core values and steps of the G4 curriculum.
- **Subject-specific group**—Where G4 participants gather to discuss progress regarding their specific struggle. The majority of time at a G4 evening is spent in these smaller groups.
- **Debrief**—The leaders-only conclusion to an evening of G4, when group facilitators gather for encouragement, prayer, and leadership enrichment training.
- **Graduation**—A celebration for when a participant has met their goal at G4 and is choosing to fully transition into the discipleship ministries of the church for their ongoing character formation.

OTHER G4 LINGO

- **Core values**—The culture-shaping priorities that every G4 group strives to uphold, regardless of subject or type of curriculum. (See chapter 4.)
- **Informed consent**—This is the process of ensuring that each G4 participant understands what kind of ministry G4 is and

what type of training a G4 leader does/doesn't have. In any counseling-related situation, it is the responsibility of the helper to ensure that the helpee understands the type of care being offered.

- **Open group model**—A style of group that allows new guests to join the group at any point in the group's life cycle. In an open group, which is the majority model at G4, group participants will be at different points on their step work journey.
- **Closed group model**—A style of group where all participants start and finish the group at the same time.
- **Sanctification**—The theological term for the process of change. Using the term sanctification implies that a Christ-like, God-honoring life is a core element of the type of change being pursued.
- **Sin/responsibility curriculum**—Curriculum that approaches its given subject from the perspective that the participant's struggle is primarily a result of their own beliefs, choices, and values. The terms *sin-based* or *responsibility-focused* are used interchangeably to designate this curriculum.
- **Suffering curriculum**—Curriculum that approaches its given subject from the perspective that the participant's struggle emerges from the effects of living in a broken world, among broken people, and within a body that is impacted by the effects of the fall.
- **Step work**—Most groups at G4 work through a curriculum comprising nine steps. Working through these steps is often called a participant's "step work."

The goal of G4 is not to teach participants a new language. The words defined in this chapter don't supercharge or accelerate the change process. As an act of hospitality, we do want to eliminate as much confusion as possible at G4. Change is hard. We want to do everything we can to remove barriers to change. Clarifying frequently used terms like these is one way we do that.

Section One: *Understanding* the Life Cycle of a Night of G4

Of the three life cycles, this one is the easiest for you to "do." If we compare a G4 ministry to a garden, this life cycle is the equivalent of tilling the soil and planting seeds—setting the garden up so that there is a place for plants to grow. The work of the other two life cycles—fostering growth in individual participants and managing the dynamics of the G4 group you lead—is like tending the garden once the seeds are in the ground. We can't make seeds sprout or plants grow. We can merely understand the conditions that facilitate plant growth best and strive to create those conditions.

In this section, we will walk through segment by segment what happens on a night of G4. If you are leading the only G4 group at your church, you should focus on chapters 6, 7, 9, and 11. As your church adds more groups, then chapters 8 and 10 will become relevant.

Chapter 6

CREATING AWARENESS AND CLARIFYING EXPECTATIONS

Groups do not auto-populate. To get from a group that is *available* but empty to a group that is *changing lives*, we must create awareness that this group exists amongst people who would benefit from this group. Furthermore, ten individuals in a room do not automatically form a group. For a meaningful group to emerge, people must have a shared set of expectations and purpose. To cultivate a cohesive G4 group, we need to communicate clearly about what this group is and what prospective members can expect. These are the twin tasks of chapter 6: *awareness* and *clarity*.

CULTIVATING AWARENESS

As you think about launching a new G4 group, ask yourself, *Where would we find the people who would benefit from this group?* Two natural places to look are in the church and in the surrounding community. We'll consider how to cultivate awareness in each sphere.

Inside the church

When we think *in the church*, we are prone to think *Sunday morning service announcement*. For the sake of your morale and the health of your relationship with your pastor(s), please realize every ministry in the church vies for this prime informational real estate. Because you don't want services to be two hours long (which is what would happen if pastors announced everything they were asked to announce), you are unlikely to get enough promotion via the Sunday morning service to sustain adequate G4 awareness.

Don't panic! Instead, think of subgroups within the church that are a good fit for your G4 group. Are you leading a men's purity group? Set up a table at the next men's conference. Are you leading a women's group for depression? Ask the women's discipleship coordinator to send out an email. Are you leading a group for blended families? Ask the children and student ministries leaders to mention it at their next parents' meeting. These examples are brainstorming prompts. Ask yourself, *Where would the people for my group already be connected in my church, and how could I most easily help leaders in those ministries share information about G4?*

Your church probably has several social media channels (Twitter, Facebook, Instagram, or whatever platform becomes popular next). Create several announcements about your group formatted for each social media type. Ask if these posts can be disseminated at a set interval (i.e., every other week or monthly) to maintain awareness within the church as a whole.

In addition, instead of asking for a Sunday morning announcement, ask how G4 can serve your pastor. What do pastors need that G4 is uniquely positioned to offer? The answer is "practical next steps." If anxiety is a theme in the sermon, in less than ten seconds and without altering the flow of the message, your pastor can say, "This is why I am glad we have a G4 group on anxiety. This would be a great next step for many of us. Check out ourchurchwebsite.com/G4 for all the groups offered through our G4 ministry." Ask your pastor to look for these opportunities when he is preparing his sermons. Schedule strategic social media posts to follow up on sermons like these.

Outside the church

It may be less instinctive to think about promotion outside the church. Ask yourself, *where do people who experience your group's struggle go for help?* Are you leading a group on eating disorders? Reach out to local nutritionists. Are you leading a group on marriage betrayal? Reach out to local marriage counselors or family law attorneys. Are you leading a group on miscarriage? Reach out to professionals who provide various forms of prenatal care.

Will every person in these roles recommend your group? No. But don't fear rejection. Raising awareness for a ministry is like fishing: You won't catch something on every cast, but it's important to keep your bait in the water. As you find believers in these spheres, they will be excited about your ministry as a way to be salt and light in their workplace. Also, they will become important resources for you to recommend to people in your group.

Don't forget that people inside your church often have the ability to reach people outside the church. Be prepared to provide church members what they need to leverage their workplaces or social groups to raise awareness. Does someone own a business with a waiting room or point of sale? Create a G4 brochure for them. Does your church have a ministry for moms of preschoolers in the community? Create a flyer that can go home in the bag with the kid's artwork. You are doing something good, and people need to know about it. Don't be weird (don't promote your trauma group by knitting pet sweaters with the G4 logo for emotional support animals), but do be creative and assertive.

CLARIFYING EXPECTATIONS

Once you cultivate awareness, you need to be a good steward of the interest you have raised. The way that you steward interest is by using *clear communication about G4* with *clear steps to connect with G4*. Awareness without clarity creates frustration.

The first part of clarity is having a clear and complete G4 page on your church website. Once this is made (and kept up-to-date), the only thing anyone—pastoral staff, church member, or community partner—needs to remember is this:

> G4 is a ministry of lay-led, subject-specific counseling groups. You can find out about active groups, meeting times, and location at ourchurchwebsite.com/G4.[1]

You need to ensure that communicating about your ministry is as simple as stating these two sentences. If people do not have this kind of ready-to-go answer when someone asks, they will begin to offer guesses about what they think your ministry ought to be (which is whatever they want it to be) and give inaccurate information to those interested in attending your group.

Who is most likely to "speak creatively" about your ministry? The answer is any pastor who mentions G4 in a sermon or Bible study. We love our pastors, but bless their hearts, when talking about church ministries, they are wonderfully notorious for making superlative statements that may not be entirely accurate. If your pastor says there is going to be a 70-foot-tall waterslide at student camp, the worst thing that happens is some teenagers are disappointed. If your pastor says "The G4 addiction group at our church has everything you need to get from detox to victory!" or "From the testimonies I hear, our G4 group on depression is so good you won't need your Prozac anymore!" it's a problem.

Pastors often use superlatives and exaggerated descriptions to affirm ministries within the church. But for a counseling ministry, these kinds of statements are not affirmations; they are false advertisements that create inaccurate expectations. Misleading information, even if well-intended, discourages people from reaching out for help (it's too good to be true) and discredits the church's counseling ministry in the eyes of your community partners. For this reason, any time your pastor is going to say something about G4 (and you hope he will frequently), he needs to know who to vet his

---

1. A sample of a church's G4 page can be found at summitchurch.com/G4.

statement with to make sure it's accurate. That person is your G4 director.

MAINTAINING CLARITY FROM THE WEBSITE TO THE FIRST NIGHT

No website will answer every question a potential participant could ask. It is important that you designate responsibility for answering questions that are not on the website. Be sure that your website has clear instructions regarding the name, email address, and/or phone number for the person to contact if there are questions. This person would be your G4 director (if you have a collection of groups), the member of the pastoral team who oversees G4, or the G4 group leader (for churches that have just a few decentralized groups).

Someone asking questions about G4 is often in a pivotal place in their life. The windows of time when someone is willing to seek help are often brief. Therefore, the response should be timely and concise and provide answers to their questions without overwhelming them with information. Be encouraging without overpromising the impact of G4. Leave room for people to be pleasantly surprised. Always provide them a warm invitation to be a part of G4's next meeting time.

Chapter 7

WELCOME: FROM THE PARKING LOT TO "HELLO"

We've all heard the axiom, "You never get a second chance to make a first impression." This is especially true when someone is uncertain or apprehensive about a choice that feels risky. For this reason, we need to lead every night of G4 like it is somebody's first night at G4.

In this chapter, we will focus primarily on first-time guests as we walk through a recommended G4 welcoming process. But a strong welcoming process isn't just about the retention of first-time guests. It is also an encouragement to the frequent attender who had a rough week and wrestled in their mind about whether it was worth coming this week.

Here is how the time of welcoming fits into the schedule of an evening of G4 if you decide your G4 evening starts at 6:30:

- 6:00—Setup begins
- 6:15—Doors open for welcoming
- 6:30—Large group
- 6:45—Break out into subject-specific groups
- 8:15—Participants depart and debrief begins
- 8:45—G4 leaders depart

Let's break down all of the important things that happen during this window.

RECOGNIZE AND GREET FIRST-TIME GUESTS

There are several "tells" that can indicate this is someone's first time at G4.

- You do not recognize them. Over time, even if you have multiple groups meeting on the same night, you will recognize the regulars.
- They are not carrying their group curriculum. People who have already been to group know they need to bring their curriculum each week. New guests haven't received a curriculum yet.
- They are timid or look lost. Once someone has been to G4 once or twice, they know to check in and make their way into large group.

Have a few G4 leaders, both male and female, at the entry of the building to greet G4 regulars and look for first-time guests. When they see someone displaying these tells, a greeter should move toward that person with a smile.

For some groups, it may be awkward for a first-time guest to be greeted by someone of the opposite gender. For example, if a female leader asks a male guest "What group can I help you find?" and he responds "The men's purity group," it can be uncomfortable. The same can be true for a female guest put in a position of telling a male leader she's looking for the women's abuse group. For that reason, encourage male leaders to greet male first-time guests and female leaders to greet female first-time guests.

INTRODUCE YOURSELF

As you move toward them, your nonverbal communication should convey that you're glad they're here. Your first goal is not to learn their name or find out what group they're interested in, but to make them feel welcome and assuage any fear about how they'll be received.

After a smile and a warm "We're so glad you're here," ask their name. Tell them your name. Let them know how long you've been coming to G4. Ask if they would like help getting connected at G4. Of course they would. But asking the question helps them feel like they're not being moved against their will.

HELP THEM REGISTER

Walk with them to the registration area, likely a table with G4 table drape[1] and a computer or tablet. The registration process covers three primary things: (a) contact information, (b) group selection, and (c) informed consent. As you explain this part of the process, you might say the following:

> "This is where we ask people to register. We ask for your contact information so we can follow up with you in the event of inclement weather and the need to cancel. We ask which group you are interested in so that a leader can give you updates on the group. And we do something called *informed consent* so people are clear about what G4 is and isn't."

After that, you allow them to walk through the registration process[2] and ask any questions they may have. If someone is unsure about which group they want to join, connect them with your G4 director or ask which group is the closest fit and take them to that group's leader for additional clarification.

In the informed consent part of registration, there are three things we want to make sure a first-time guest understands

1. At www.johnhchapman.com/G4setupmaterials you can find links to order materials that churches frequently use to set up an evening of G4. We do not profit from these materials, but we have coordinated with vendors to make these materials easily available. Please feel free to use connections with local vendors if your church has those established relationships.
2. A sample registration process can be found at www.johnhchapman.com/G4registration.

about G4. You need to know what these are so you can respond accurately to questions a guest may have as they register. In the following paragraphs, we will discuss these three important things.

First, G4 is not professional counseling. Many people hear the word *counseling* and think *professional.* We want people to know that G4 is a lay-led ministry. Our leaders have personal experience with the struggles for which they lead a group, but they do not have advanced academic training as counselors.

Second, G4 is not trying to replace individual counseling. Some participants are already meeting with a professional counselor. That's great. Some may want to pursue individual counseling in addition to G4. That's no problem. Some are content to only participate in G4. If we can adequately meet their needs, that's fine too.

Third, at G4 we strive to uphold confidentiality. In a lay-based, group counseling ministry, confidentiality is not as straightforward as it is with a professional counselor. We ask participants to honor each other's stories like they want their story to be honored. G4 leaders do not share a participant's information, even with pastors within the church, without permission from that participant. But we cannot guarantee confidentiality because there are other participants in the room that we do not control. This is a generally accepted risk in all group-based counseling settings.

GIVE THEM CURRICULUM

After your guest registers, take them to get the curriculum for their group. You should have curriculum for each group in a designated area that is easily accessible to volunteers. Some churches will budget to provide free curriculum to each participant. Other churches will ask participants to reimburse the church for the cost of the curriculum. This is a relatively small, one-time expense.

Receiving a curriculum can be intimidating. But you can reduce a new participant's apprehension by reassuring them that only a small portion of the curriculum is covered each week and that each participant moves at their own pace. It is often helpful to mention that the group leader will explain how the curriculum is used in their specific group.

HAVE YOUR GUEST SIGN IN

This is where your guest will begin their evening at G4 in subsequent weeks; this is the start of a "normal" week at G4. Two simple things happen at sign in. First, each participant verifies attendance so the ministry has an attendance record. Second, each participant puts on a name tag, ensuring each person can be addressed by name in group.

INTRODUCE THEM TO THEIR GROUP LEADER

Until this point, the new participant has been your participant. At this point, you will hand the new participant off to their group leader. This group leader should take the participant into the large group space and answer any remaining questions that have not been previously answered. This is also the time when their new G4 leader begins having the conversations we will discuss in chapters 12 and 18. Your guest has been welcomed, and now we have set the stage for our large group discussion.

Chapter 8

LARGE GROUP: REINFORCING THE CULTURE OF G4

At G4, large group is brief but significant. If executed well, large group should take no more than fifteen minutes. Teaching during large group is not profound and doesn't try to stir our emotions. Large group's rhythm is predictable. But large group reinforces the culture of G4 and allows G4 to remain a cohesive ministry as its individual groups address a wide variety of topics.

If you only have one G4 group at your church, you will not have a large group time. You will need to find other ways to accomplish the benefits discussed in this chapter. But once you have multiple groups, large group helps maintain a shared culture within the ministry.

During large group, you will accomplish three things:

1. PROVIDE A BUFFER BETWEEN LIFE AND GROUP

For everyone—leaders, committed group members, and first-time guests—large group provides a cognitive and emotional buffer between the workday, getting dinner, hustling to G4, and the beginning of group. This may seem minor, but enabling participants to arrive at their subject-specific groups with settled minds and a timely reminder of what G4 is about has a major impact.

During large group time, guests can acclimate to being at G4. They can listen and learn before they share and receive feedback. Seeing the number of people present gives participants the comfort of knowing that they are not alone in their struggle.

For first-time guests, the physical layout of large group is intentional. We recommend setting chairs up in rows rather than in a circle because when you are working up the courage to be vulnerable, rows are less intimidating than circles. In a circle, you are making eye contact with everyone. By contrast, in rows, everyone is facing front.

With a good welcoming process (chapter 7), a guest can sit with their new G4 facilitator, get to know the leader a bit better, ask questions, and thereby begin to cultivate trust they can take into their subject-specific group. Walking into group with someone they have been introduced to makes the transition to their subject-specific group less intimidating.

Further, beginning the evening program with large group allows everyone to enter their subject-specific group at the same time. This helps the new participant not to feel like all eyes are on them as they walk into the room. This helps established members avoid an awkward starting and restarting of vulnerable disclosures about their growth as more people enter the room.

2. GIVE PARTICIPANTS FAMILIARITY WITH G4 LEADERSHIP

We have mentioned that the G4 facilitator is not a personal counselor for each individual in the group. Large group helps reinforce this expectation in the mind of participants. Each week, everyone sees that G4 has leaders (plural) and not just a group leader (singular). This is a distinctly different feel from entering a counseling setting at a private practice, where everyone has their own counselor.

As participants enter the building, they are greeted by other G4 group leaders and established group members. At check-in, they meet more leaders. When large group starts, the G4 director greets the crowd and does much of the teaching, but other G4 group leaders may also share the microphone.

Seeing other leaders and having established rhythms breaks the expectation that "my leader should do whatever I need them to do," which can often emerge in a church-based counseling ministry. It becomes clear that G4 is a ministry with processes and protocols. Care is given in an established way that is sustainable for leaders and protects participants. Where order is present, people are less prone to impose their own expectations.

3. HELP PARTICIPANTS UNDERSTAND G4 VALUES AND MODELS

You should notice that in the first two points, we didn't mention the content of the teaching given during large group. That doesn't mean the teaching content during large group is unimportant. We put this point third because we want you to appreciate the non-teaching benefits of large group.

Now we will walk through the two primary teaching elements of large group. Each week during large group, the G4 director, or someone they've enlisted, will teach on *either* one of the seven core values *or* one of the nine steps. A welcome and any ministry-wide announcements (e.g., how you'll manage G4 meeting times during a holiday season like Thanksgiving) are also made during this time.

This means twice per year you will cover all seven core values and both sets of nine steps. The formula is as follows:

- seven values + nine steps (sin) + nine steps (suffering) = twenty-five topics
- twenty-five topics x two cycles = fifty weeks (with fifty-two weeks in each year)

Core values

In chapter 4, we defined the seven core values of G4:

1. G4 is Bible-based and gospel-centered.
2. G4 recognizes the difference between sin and suffering.
3. G4 is built on honesty and transparency.
4. G4 upholds confidentiality.

5. G4 avoids struggle-based identity.
6. G4 blends discipleship, accountability, and a guided process.
7. G4 transitions into the church's discipleship ministries.

For these values to become culture instead of principles that only exist on paper, they need to be discussed regularly. The description of each value provides the key content to cover for each core value during large group.

Through this ongoing reinforcement of G4's core values and steps, large group becomes the ongoing informed consent of G4. When a new participant comes to G4, they read these seven core values as they register. Hearing these values repeated and explained serves as a reminder of what they agreed to be a part of. Repetition reinforces the standard you are calling all groups to adhere to. Each time you teach on a core value, you are simultaneously conveying, "This is who we commit to be *for* you, and this is what we expect *from* you toward each other."

Nine-step models

In chapters 13 and 14, we cover the nine steps for sin and the nine steps for suffering. Every person is simultaneously both sinner and sufferer; we sin, and we are affected by living in a broken world. This means that every participant needs both sanctification models. Covering both models in large group reminds us of this truth. Additionally, for groups using non-G4 curriculums, hearing these two models taught helps participants contextualize their curriculum within these sanctification models (see the guidance on how to use other types of curriculum in chapter 15).

During their subject-specific groups, participants will get "down in the weeds" of each step as they work through their curriculum. Succinctly covering each step during large group allows participants see the big picture of their journey. Both the aerial view and the view from the ground are needed to maintain morale and progress.

A BASIC SCHEDULE FOR LARGE GROUP

Each large group should have the same rhythm. Rhythm allows participants to transition more effectively from a workday mindset to a G4 mindset. While the content of large group will change, the structure should remain the same. If G4 starts at 6:30 at your church, here is a recommended schedule for what we've covered so far:

- 6:15—Doors open to participants
- 6:30—Large Group Begins
    - » Welcome and announcements (2–3 minutes)
    - » Teaching a core value or one of the nine steps (7–10 minutes)
    - » Concluding prayer (2–3 minutes)
- 6:45—Send participants to their subject-specific group

These times are approximations and may vary. It is most important to remember that the large group exists to serve the subject-specific groups. Large group time isn't the "star" of G4, even though it has the biggest audience. Large group gets everyone to their small groups at the same time, with common expectations, and in a good mindset to engage their topic.

Chapter 9

SUBJECT-SPECIFIC GROUPS: WORKING ON LIFE STRUGGLES

This is the longest chapter in section one. That's appropriate, because subject-specific groups are the most central part of an evening at G4. As a G4 facilitator, leading your subject-specific group is what you will most prepare for each week.

As an evening of G4 transitions from large group to subject-specific groups, the topics being discussed get narrower. In large group, we discuss things everyone has in common: core values and the nine-step models. In subject-specific groups, we talk about our specific struggles: addiction, depression, trauma, or other topics. More specifically, we talk about our personal journeys with one of these struggles.

Ironically, in subject-specific groups, while the topic gets narrower, each person's journey gets more varied. In large group, everyone is learning the same thing at the same time. A large-group topic like honoring confidentiality looks the same for everyone at G4. But in subject-specific groups, each participant may be at a different place in their personal journey. Furthermore, application of a particular step may look different for people even if they are in the same group.

To prepare you to lead your subject-specific group, we'll cover the following four subjects in this chapter:

1. setting a tentative schedule;
2. facilitating the curriculum;
3. sharing step work and giving accountability; and
4. leading effective prayer times

SETTING A TENTATIVE SCHEDULE

As you think about your group's schedule, here is the tension. No two weeks at G4 will look alike. But after a few weeks, everyone should know what to expect. We balance this tension by having a base schedule that gets implemented with flexibility. Depending on your curriculum and the size of your group, the order of the schedule and the time allotment for each segment may vary. You are fully deputized to make adjustments, as long as you accomplish the objectives of each component. What must be accomplished includes:

- Welcome and orienting new guests
- Personal updates (5–10 minutes)
- Facilitating and sharing (30–40 minutes). These two segments often meld together, although we cover them separately in this chapter.
    - » Covering a step or step segment (10–15 minutes)—G4 facilitator leads discussion
    - » Personal step work progress and accountability (20–25 minutes)—G4 participants report
- Prayer (5–10 minutes)

1. Welcome and orienting new guests

If you are leading the only G4 group at your church, you will need to emphasize the importance of people arriving on time. Timeliness honors the other participants and maximizes your time together. Once you have multiple G4 groups, large group helps ensure that everyone arrives to your group at the same time.

During these first few minutes, you will help guests get oriented to the group and help the group assimilate first-time guests effectively (chapter 18). This is also the time when you can address housekeeping matters for your group that have emerged in recent weeks.

2. Personal updates

Immediately jumping into the work of G4 can make the group feel impersonal and inadvertently stifle the level of vulnerability that fosters change. Allowing a few minutes for major life updates creates a sense of mutual care and awareness within the group. Even if no one has an update that week, asking communicates that each participant is more than their struggle. It humanizes the group. You may have a few over-sharers you need to rein in during this time (chapter 16), but humanizing the group is worth it.

3. Facilitating and sharing

Covering a step or step segment: The group facilitator leads this time. Most groups will walk sequentially through their curriculum from week to week. The goal for this segment is to familiarize participants with the journey as a whole. The discussion may focus on a whole step, a part of a step, or a designated unit of material in a non-nine-step curriculum. While the facilitator comes prepared to prompt the group with questions, the bulk of this time should be discussion through the content of the curriculum.

Personal step work progress and accountability: After the group discusses a section of curriculum, each participant is invited to update the group on their weekly progress. Although this sharing time shouldn't be strictly regimented, it should follow this basic outline:

- My name is . . .
- I am currently working on step number . . .
- As I studied this week, I learned . . .
- As I strove to make progress, I did . . .
- This week my biggest challenge toward progress was . . .

In addition, each person's sharing time needs to be succinct, unless it was a pivotal week for them. Sharing succinctly is important because if group morphs into a meeting lasting two or three hours, you will have a hard time retaining members. To keep things moving, you want to create an expectation among participants that they will share each week so that they give forethought to what they will share during this time. Forethought allows members to share in a meaningful way without excessive time to say it.

4. Prayer

Finally, having a time of prayer gives closure to the evening, provides an opportunity for participants to minister to one another through prayer, and settles the minds of each participant as they reengage with life outside of G4. The weightiness of what is wrestled with in G4 makes this emotional buffer important.

FACILITATING THE CURRICULUM

Leading a G4 group doesn't mean you have to be an expert in the subject matter the group is addressing. G4 is structured to take that pressure off you. You have the title "G4 facilitator" rather than "lay counselor" to help establish an accurate expectation in your mind and the minds of your group participants.

A video-based teaching supplements the written curriculum of the nine-step G4 curriculum.[1] This helps remove the pressure for you to be a subject matter expert. These videos can serve to preview steps for new group members, refresh the memories of not-so-new members, and encourage all members as they work their way through the curriculum.

The purpose of your teaching is to *shepherd* more than *educate* the group. With that in mind, let's explore three emphases for this segment of your group's life.

Work through the curriculum sequentially.

Begin at the beginning and slowly work your way forward. When a group is first formed, participants will be working the

1. The accompanying videos are available for free at bradhambrick.com. See appendix A for specific links to each G4 nine-step curriculum.

steps in sync with your teaching. As the group matures, some members will work the steps more slowly and new members will arrive. This means that, in time, the teaching segment and personal updates will not be synchronized, which is fine.

As you work sequentially through the curriculum, focus on how each step builds on the previous steps and sets up the next step. Your goal is to make each step seem less staccato. Working through a G4 curriculum is not like studying a book in college. *Participants are not mastering content; they are walking a journey*. Lead the discussion in a way that helps participants make this cognitive shift from content to journey.

Teach in a way that values private study.

Practically, this means assigning specific pages for participants to read each week. When participants read the assigned content, it allows you to use a more questions-based approach. Verbally summarizing the material in response to your questions helps participants "own" the material by putting it into their words. As this shift happens, you can focus on shepherding how participants are applying the curriculum, as opposed to merely repeating to them the content of the curriculum. A questions-based approach also draws on the experience of more tenured members of the group.

When first-time guests are present, explain to them the difference between *reading* for the group discussion and *working* the steps for personal growth.

Reading assigned pages is for familiarity. On any given week, this should take less than thirty minutes. A participant can read material from step 5 for understanding, even if they are still working on step 2 for application.

Working the steps is for growth and change. Participants should spend several hours each week working on this task in daily increments. Just because a participant has read a section and watched the videos does not mean they have completed the step. They have completed the step when the change represented in that step has been achieved in their life.

Teach in a way that prompts authenticity.

Each week you want to prime the pump for honesty by how you facilitate this discussion. That might entail the following:

- Sharing how you were challenged while reviewing this material.
- Being honest about what was hard for you when implementing this material in your personal journey.
- Giving examples of how you've admired past participants who wrestled with implementing this section of material.

As the group leader, your voice sets the tone and culture for how participants will share about their personal progress and challenges. *That means that the best G4 facilitator is not the most eloquent teacher, but the teacher who draws out greater authenticity from participants*. As you prepare each week, you want to be asking yourself, *How can I review this material with the humility and transparency that I want my group members to mirror as they give personal updates?*

SHARING STEP WORK AND GIVING ACCOUNTABILITY

Earlier, we gave a five-part outline for this sharing time (see p. 47). We will review that outline in more detail here, but don't allow this outline to become formulaic. Understanding the importance of each point helps the group use the outline without feeling robotic.

Newer members may initially choose to cover only a few of these points. That is fine. In time, they will share more. But established members should begin to naturally organize their thoughts with this outline.

Each group member needs to be aware of the time. An outline like this helps members share effectively and efficiently. The amount of time each participant can share is impacted by the number of people in the group. But updates should take three to five minutes, unless there was a major event in the participant's life that week.

Let's consider the five parts of the outline in detail.

1. My name is . . .

We share our name because we want to create an expectation that new people will be present each week. This isn't merely a group-growth strategy, although it has that effect; it also serves as a perpetual reminder that G4 is an open group ministry. Being in the habit of saying our name each time we share creates a culture that is less disrupted when new participants arrive.

2. I am on step number . . .

Remember, in a G4 group each participant may be on a different step, so members of the group will be sharing from different places on their journey. Declaring what step we are working on helps others in the group know how to relate to what is being shared. If someone is sharing about an earlier step, experienced members know to reflect back on that part of their journey as they listen. If someone is sharing about a later step, newer members know to try to glean some helpful material in advance of their own journey.

Additionally, it is important to remember that someone might work on the same step for several weeks, perhaps a month or more. And after a participant has a significant setback, they may decide to return to an earlier step and resume work they had previously considered complete. For this reason, you may need to occasionally remind members that G4 is not a nine-week program with completion of one step per week. That would be a book study for education, rather than a counseling group for growth.

Giving a weekly update on which step we are working on maintains an expectation of growth. We don't want to rush one another. G4 is not a race among participants. However, we do want to disavow the notion that merely showing up each week counts as "doing G4." G4 is something each participant does all week; group time is merely when we update one another on our progress and challenges.

3. This week I learned . . .

In sharing their insights, participants are not reteaching the step they are working on; instead, they are giving testimony to their learning experience. Here are five types of insight a participant might commonly share during this time:

- I learned something *about myself*. We want G4 participants to grow in self-awareness.
- I learned something *about my struggle*. We want G4 participants to become more informed about their struggle.
- I learned something *about God*. We want G4 participants to get to know God as they wrestle with their struggle.
- I learned something *about the Bible*. When participants can connect these first three areas of learning with specific Bible passages, we get excited. We want to foster this kind of growth.
- I learned something *about my struggle's impact on others*. We want G4 participants to be other-minded even as they work on their personal struggle.

When you as a G4 facilitator orient new participants to this part of group life, this is an excellent time to review these five prompts. The rest of the group may not even realize that you are shaping what they share as they listen to you orient the new member, but as you repeat these themes it will influence what is shared.

At G4, we want to affirm insight development, but we do not want to mistake insight for change. That is why "what I learned" and "how I strove to make progress" are two separate sharing prompts. Insight is a foundation for change, but it is not the same thing as change.

Most often the time a participant spends sharing their insights should be briefer than the time they spend sharing about the progress they have made. At this insight stage, a participant shares enough about what they learned to account for how that resulted in their actions toward change.

4. This week I strove to make progress by . . .

Being a good G4 member means trying. And trying means we will sometimes fail—or at least it may take several attempts at trying something new before we begin to do it well. G4 is a context where we encourage one another in this striving. At G4 we would rather try and fail than not try and stay the same.

Why do we emphasize striving? Because it's important for each G4 participant to be able to share every week both what they learned and how they tried to implement what they learned. This weekly sharing rhythm makes James 1:22–25 a reality in your group:

> But be doers of the word, and not hearers only, deceiving yourselves. For if anyone is a hearer of the word and not a doer, he is like a man who looks intently at his natural face in a mirror. For he looks at himself and goes away and at once forgets what he was like. But the one who looks into the perfect law, the law of liberty, and perseveres, being no hearer who forgets but a doer who acts, he will be blessed in his doing.

What each person shares during this time will be unique due to the struggle your group focuses on, the step a participant is working on, and the distinctive factors in their life. But each person should be able to communicate how insights are translating into actions.

5. This week my biggest challenge has been . . .

This prompt is what might be more classically thought of as accountability. When was I tempted? When did my motivation wane? How have I sought to be less authentic with people in my support network? Did I have a setback this week?

The expectation to be active does not come with the naive belief that change is easy. If we ended with the progress prompt, it might imply that we thought change was linear; that is, simple and uninterrupted. But we want to invite a greater level of honesty than that. Honesty in the context of trusted relationships is one of the most powerful parts of G4. A commitment to change is a commitment to being honest. As G4 facilitators, we want to perpetually remind our groups of this reality.

In many ways, you can measure the health of your group by the vulnerability of responses as members discuss their biggest challenge of the week. The courage to openly acknowledge challenges reveals trust in the group.

We want G4 to be a place where we rely on God's strength by being willing to acknowledge our weaknesses (2 Corinthians 12:8–10). When we don't verbalize our challenges, we are, at least, giving the impression we have our life together, and more likely, beginning to believe we can change in our own strength. When we acknowledge our challenges, we are inviting the help of God and our friends.

LEADING EFFECTIVE PRAYER TIMES

The more faithfully each participant ends their step work update by sharing the challenges they currently face, the more naturally you will be able to segue into this final part of group time. The honest sharing will make clear what needs to be prayed about for each person in the circle.

You want to make sure that prayer time does not become a stale closing ritual. One way to prevent this is to vary how prayer time is conducted. Below are some suggestions:

- As the leader, you might pray for each person by name and mention the challenges they're facing.
- You might ask each participant to pray for the person on their right or left.
- You might ask each participant to pray about something related to the step they are currently working for the group.
- You might ask each person to pray for growth in a character quality that makes the group effective (honesty, transparency, trust, endurance, the absence of shame, etc.).
- You might ask each person to pray for the friends and family members outside of G4 who are an important part of their support network.

Brainstorm what approaches fit your group best. This list is not exhaustive but is meant to be a prompt for creativity. Both the topic of your group and where your group is in its collective life cycle (section three) may impact how you approach this time.

The goal is to prevent praying from becoming a mindless task at the end of the meeting. You want to give prompts that invite each person to intentionally engage with God for something specific. Periodically, it is important to remind the group: "We are asking God to do what we could not do and that's why we're here. We are at G4 because we need God's help in this specific area of our life. We pray to remind ourselves of that and to ask God to make real or make effective the things that we've talked about tonight."

If you give this charge too often, it loses its effect. But if you get a sense that the Godwardness of your group is waning into rhythmic rituals, this kind of admonition prior to prayer time can be an effective reminder.

REVIEWING A NIGHT AT G4

As you are concluding this chapter, review the tentative schedule for a group meeting.

- Welcome and orienting new guests
- Personal updates (5–10 minutes)
- Facilitating and sharing (30–40 minutes). These are often done simultaneously or in either order. You are fully deputized to lead your group as serves your group best.
    - Covering a step or step segment (10–15 minutes)
    - Personal step work progress and accountability (20–25 minutes)
- Prayer (5–10 minutes)

Ask yourself the following questions about each component: *Do I know what this component contributes to the life of the group? Do I know my role in leading this component? Could I walk through this schedule if I had my notes to teach on the step we are focusing on in group this week?* If so, you are ready to manage the logistics of leading your group, which fulfills this chapter's purpose.

Chapter 10

DEBRIEF: CARING FOR YOUR G4 LEADERS

In section one, we are orienting you to an evening at G4. As a group facilitator, you have more responsibilities in some parts of an evening of G4 than others. For instance, you have more responsibilities during the subject-specific group time than in large group. But it is important for you to understand the purpose and structure of each part of an evening at G4.

As we discuss debrief, it will feel more like our discussion of large group. Your G4 director has the primary responsibility to lead during this time, but the more you understand the importance of this time the more benefit you will get from it . . . and debrief is all about caring for you!

In the early weeks of a new G4 ministry, G4 leaders will use debrief to discuss how they did during the group session and what they can do to refine it for next week. But once the ministry gets established, you will need to plan for this time.

Debrief is another segment, like large group, that is relatively brief but has significant value. A well-run debrief can be the difference between leaders who burn out after six months and leaders who are thriving after six years. A common evening of G4 looks like this:

- 6:00—Setup for the evening begins
- 6:15—Doors open for welcoming
- 6:30—Large group
- 6:45—Break out into subject-specific groups
- **8:15—Participants depart and debrief begins**
- **8:45—G4 leaders depart**

In this chapter, we are going to consider how to steward these twenty to thirty minutes to make G4 a sustainable experience for leaders and to provide ongoing training to equip leaders to be more effective group facilitators.

HAVE A PLAN

If a G4 director wants leaders to value this time, there needs to be a plan. Group facilitators need to know what they will get from this time and why it's important for them. However, if the director is creating a fresh plan every week, they will burn out. That is the reason it is recommended that your G4 ministry create a monthly rhythm. This helps your director prepare and lets the leaders know what to expect.

The following list gives a possible monthly rhythm for the debrief time:

- Week one—collective prayer
- Week two—G4 enrichment training
- Week three—stories of growth
- Week four—food and fellowship
- Week five—outside speakers (when a month has a fifth week)

Regardless of the focus of a given debrief, always ask, "Is there a challenge we need to discuss?"

For the remainder of this chapter the "you" shifts from G4 facilitator to G4 director. As a facilitator-in-training, you are eavesdropping on the instructions for debrief. We hope this heightens your appreciation and enthusiasm for this time. Now let's examine in depth each element in the monthly rhythm.

Collective prayer

Your leaders need a prayer time that they don't lead. Debrief can provide this. Invite prayer requests that aren't related to their group. Does your addiction group leader have a child who is struggling in math? Does your trauma leader have a parent in the hospital? Is your depression leader moving into a new home and feeling overwhelmed by the logistics? Pray for these things that likely don't get brought up in their G4 group.

When leaders get cared for as people, not just as leaders, it makes ministry more sustainable. It protects against the resentments that build up when life is hard by fostering a sense of community among your G4 leaders. The prayer week each month should be a time of nurturing your leaders. As requests are made, write them down so that you can follow up on situations your leaders ask for prayer about. This is a small way of caring for your team, but it will make a tremendous difference.

G4 enrichment training

The G4 enrichment training component of debrief provides for G4 leaders what large group provides for G4 participants. It is a time to regularly review important content to maintain and enrich your ministry culture. The content for enrichment week will usually be a review of a chapter from *Mobilizing* or *Facilitating*.[1]

Yes, your leaders will have read *Facilitating* as part of their initial orientation, but after they've been leading for six months, they will get something new from the material. It is like premarital counseling: it should be done before you get married, but after you've been married for a year, you can go back to that same material and glean a lot more from it.

---

1. For training beyond *Mobilizing* and *Facilitating* see www.johnhchapman.com/debrieftopics for both topics and links to articles with content to cover during this time.

Discussing this material allows your more experienced leaders to share the wisdom they've garnered. This expands the number of leaders you have in your ministry. When experienced leaders see how much they've grown, it encourages them. Newer leaders get the advantage of not having to learn every lesson the hard way. Creating a context for these conversations is good stewardship of the growing leadership experience you have in your G4 ministry.

Stories of growth

People volunteer to lead in G4 to see lives changed. That's why there is nothing (and we rarely use emphatic statements like this) that motivates your leaders like hearing the stories of changed lives. These stories can be shared without breaching G4's core value of confidentiality. Leaders might say things like the following examples:

- "We've had three new people join our group this month and each one seems to have the commitment level to stick with the group. Seeing new people join has been really encouraging for our established members."
- "In our anger group, one of our guys who had been written up at work twice for rudeness with customers won the employee of the month award. When the boss asked him what made the difference in his life, he told him about G4, walked him through the nine steps, and shared the gospel with him. He said his boss might come to church this weekend."
- "Our trauma group has gotten connected with the chaplain for the police department. The chaplain is well connected with local EMTs and the fire department. There are several believers there who were excited about what we're doing. They want to come to our group a few times and see if they can launch something similar at their church."
- "In our addiction group, one of our members who has been there for a couple of months teared up during group last week

> and said this was the safest place she's ever been and that she looks forward to G4 all week. This prompted everybody in group to comment on how appreciative they were to have somewhere they could be honest and wrestle with the process of change. It was a really sweet moment for our group."

Names and identifying information are not needed to highlight how lives are being changed. After someone shares, create a culture of celebration: clap, shout, or say Amen! These kinds of stories merit more than a solemn response. Respond to these stories with the enthusiasm they deserve to energize your leaders. Ask another group leader to pray a prayer of thanksgiving for the positive results in this other group. Create a culture where each G4 leader is a cheerleader for successes in the other groups.

Food and fellowship

It is good for your leaders to have downtime together. It doesn't need to be elaborate. Have a local restaurant cater a nacho bar. Bring ice cream and allow leaders to make sundaes. Or invite people to bring their favorite appetizer.

If prayer is spiritually nourishing, training refines the ministry, and stories of changed lives are motivating, then casual time filled with laughter is refreshingly normal and replenishing. Debrief can be used to create these refreshingly normal moments that are good for your leaders.

Outside speakers

Bringing in an outside speaker is a great way to offer a fresh voice to your leaders and cement relationships with trusted community partners. Here are some examples of connections that may yield speakers for debrief:

- Have you gotten to know a nutritionist via your eating disorder group? Invite them to speak on the role of physical health in emotional health and resilience.

- Have you gotten connected with a psychiatrist via your depression group? Invite them to do a lay-level introduction to how psychotropic medications work and common misconceptions.
- Have you gotten to know a marriage counselor through your purity and betrayal groups? Invite them to come and provide training on conflict resolution.

These kinds of trainings have both direct and indirect benefit for your leaders. The *direct benefit* is the training itself. Your leaders will become better equipped. The *indirect benefit* is the sense of assurance that emerges from realizing that their G4 director is building contacts with professionals who can help troubleshoot hard situations that emerge in group.

Inviting an outside speaker is also an effective way to network your ministry within the community. When a professional gets to see your ministry, they can recommend it to their clients more accurately. When they are talking with their professional peers about free options in the community, this professional can recommend your ministry more heartily when they've met your leaders and seen how their professional expertise was valued.

CONCLUSION

When thinking through debrief, two questions should drive your thinking. First, and most important, how can I encourage our leaders and help them maintain the emotional resilience a ministry like G4 requires? Use debrief to steward the morale of your team. If you wait until your leaders are threadbare to become intentional, maintaining leaders will be much more difficult.

Second, what type of training would help our leaders become more skilled as group facilitators? Often, this won't mean finding new content to teach. It can be as simple as reviewing the existing trainings—*Mobilizing* and *Facilitating*—and allowing your leaders to share their experience of implementing these concepts.

In this chapter, we've provided a framework with variety and rhythm so that you can have consistent debrief meetings without extensive preparation. Take this template. Make it your own. Adjust it as needed. Shape debrief in the way *that best serves your leaders*.

Chapter 11

JOB DESCRIPTION OF A G4 DIRECTOR

We've talked a lot about the role of the G4 director, the person who oversees and coordinates your G4 ministry. To wrap up our overview of a night of G4, we will succinctly summarize this role in the form of a job description.

If you are a prospective G4 group leader, please don't skip this chapter because it's important to know what a director does. If you are leading the only G4 group at your church, this chapter will familiarize you with what to watch for when your groups multiply and your groups need a G4 director. If your ministry already has a director, this information will familiarize you with how to support this person, as well as how they can support you.

The **G4 director** is the person—usually a volunteer—who is responsible to care for G4 facilitators, ensure an evening of G4 runs smoothly, and be the initial contact point for G4 facilitators when a difficult situation emerges in their group. The title "director" is not important. At your church, this person might use the title "catalyst" or "ministry champion." We chose the term *director* to indicate that this is the person who oversees the weekly operations of G4 at your church.

Early in the life of your G4 ministry, your G4 director will likely also be a group leader. When the ministry is small, the role of director is less demanding. But as the ministry grows, your G4 director will have the sole role of leading the ministry as a whole. The job description below applies in both situations.

TRAINING

The training process for the G4 director is composed of two things: First, the G4 director has read *Mobilizing* with the leadership of your church and walked through the implementation process it describes for launching G4. Second, the G4 director has read *Facilitating* and is familiar enough with the process of leading a G4 group to orient prospective group leaders to their role. In addition, webinar and in-person training events for G4 directors are available.[1]

THE G4 DIRECTOR AND THE CHURCH ORGANIZATION CHART

Understanding where your G4 director fits on the **church organization chart** and what type of communication should occur across the chart is important. The following bullet points specify communication channels for those involved in G4 ministry:

- *Your G4 director reports to the pastor—or in a church with multiple pastors, to the one who has the primary responsibility for overseeing G4 and encouraging its leadership.* The communication between this pastor and the director focuses on care for the G4 director and needs of the G4 ministry (things like additional meeting rooms, strategies for building awareness within the church, identifying potential new G4 leaders, etc.).
- *G4 facilitators report to the G4 director.* Initially the communication between a leader and the director focuses on training and orientation for the new leader. After new leaders are oriented, the G4 director provides ongoing support, encouragement, and advice on unique or hard situations in group.
- *The G4 director is the liaison between G4 facilitators and your counseling consultant.* When advice from a professional

1. An up-to-date schedule for upcoming trainings can be found at bradhambrick.com/events.

counselor is needed, the G4 director serves as the contact point between the G4 ministry and the professional counselor. Appendix B in *Facilitating* explains how you should communicate these needs with your director and what to expect. Chapter 17 in *Mobilizing* provides your director with detailed guidance on establishing and appropriately utilizing this consulting relationship.

KEY RESPONSIBILITIES

The **key responsibilities** of a G4 director follow:

- *Coordinate the recruitment and training of new G4 leaders.* This work entails interviewing potential G4 leaders, answering their initial questions, vetting their fit for this ministry, walking them through the *Facilitating* training material, and helping them identify a curriculum for their group.
- *Support and equip existing G4 leaders.* Most of this role is accomplished through a well-run weekly debriefing at the end of an evening of G4 (see chapter 10). But it also includes helping leaders think through difficult situations in groups, clarifying unclear expectations, helping leaders contextualize curriculum for their group members, and caring for leaders as people, not leaders only.
- *Ensure that an evening of G4 runs smoothly.* Each part of the schedule for an evening of G4 requires planning and coordination. The G4 director ensures that the necessary rooms are reserved, there are assigned roles for the welcoming process, the teaching segment of large group is assigned (if another leader is speaking), there is a plan for setting up subject-specific rooms (if necessary), and debrief is coordinated.
- *Serve as liaison between G4 and church leadership.* Your pastoral staff needs to know who to talk to if they have a question about G4. That person is the G4 director. Your G4 facilitators need to know who to talk to if they need something from the pastoral staff. That person is the G4 director. By having a single communication point, you prevent

confusion, redundancy, or breaches of confidentiality from emerging between G4 facilitators and church leadership.

- *Serve as liaison between G4 and the counseling consultant.* For the same reasons, the G4 director is also the sole communication point between G4 group leaders and the professional counseling consultant. Again, for a basic discussion of the relationship between G4 and the counseling consultant, see appendix B. A more robust discussion of this relationship can be found in chapter 17 of *Mobilizing*.
- *Coordinate G4's community impact strategy*. When a community partner—such as a professional counselor or a social worker—wants to know more about G4, the G4 director should be their point of contact. As G4 facilitators are brainstorming community partners that would be relevant for their group, the G4 director is the person who guides these interactions to ensure there is consistency and clarity of communication about the ministry. The G4 director also coordinates with outside professionals who may come teach during the debrief time.

As we conclude section one, you have the mental scaffolding for a night at G4. You know the key components of G4 and the intended benefits from how each component was designed. That prepares you for section two, where we will focus on the experience and growth of group participants at G4.

Section Two: *Supporting* the Life Cycle of Group Participants

In section two we will trace the life cycle of a G4 group participant. This life cycle is why G4 exists. It is primary. The other two life cycles exist to cultivate momentum and perseverance for this life cycle. Your goal in reading this section is to see the big picture of what you're praying God will do in the life of each person who attends G4.

Chapter 12

FROM ATTENDANCE TO COMMITMENT

It is easy to assume that everyone who asks for help wants to change, or that everyone who shows up to G4 wants the benefits of being part of a group. While these are understandable assumptions, if you embrace them, you will be a frustrated G4 facilitator. For this reason, we'll help you prepare to walk with someone from their first night at G4 to committing to your group.

As you think about this challenge, you likely sense a tension. New guests and established members have different needs. As the group leader, you'll be serving both at the same time. This chapter will help you balance orienting first-time guests with helping established group members maintain their progress. When you have a plan, balancing these two needs is not as complicated as you might fear.

Your goal with first-time guests is welcoming and caring for them in a way that increases the likelihood of them becoming committed members of your group. You also want to clarify what G4 is about so that they have a clear picture of what they are committing to. How to effectively accomplish these two goals is the focus of this chapter.

WELCOMING WELL

Introducing a new participant into a preexisting group can be a challenge. If we're not careful, joining an established G4 group can feel like entering a friendship clique. Everyone else already knows each other, understands the social rules, and has shared expectations for what will happen. The goal of a good welcome is to remove these relational obstacles for your first-time guests.

New participants should feel welcomed by the group, not just the group leader. They should have an opportunity, if they desire, to share a portion of their story. Welcomes should be simple and rhythmic. Your guest should feel like introductions have happened before and are an enjoyable ritual, valued by the entire group. This simplicity and predictability ensure that welcoming a guest does not consume too much group time. With this in mind, let's look at **a three-stage welcome.**

Stage one: Introduce yourself as the leader.

If your group is part of a larger G4 ministry, you will likely have met the guest during check-in and gotten to know them a bit before large group time. When you get to group, this allows you to say something like the following:

> "This is [name]. I've gotten to know him/her a bit and am excited [name] is here. I told him/her we would take a few minutes before we get started to help [name] get to know us and what G4 is about. Most of you know my story, but reshaping stories like mine is why we're here so I'm happy to share it again. [Give a short version of your story in two to three minutes and explain why you're excited to lead in G4.]"

This introduction does several things. First, calling your guest by name several times creates a sense of welcome and belonging.

Smile and make eye contact the first time you say their name. Second, it frames your guest's presence as a good thing. That is the essence of a "welcome." Third, sharing your story models authenticity and honesty. From a guest's first moments in group, we want to establish the sense that G4 is a safe place to talk about hard things.

One of the most immediate ways to garner commitment is to share your passion for the ministry. That's why it is important to incorporate into your introduction the reasons you first came to G4. Your testimony is an indirect way to cast the vision of G4.

Stage two: Ask other members to introduce themselves.

For smaller groups of three to five participants, it is possible for each group member to take one to two minutes to introduce themselves. These introductions should follow the style of your introduction—sharing a quick overview of their story and why they value G4. These introductions cultivate more hope and buy-in from the guest by giving them a glimpse into the lives of people with a variety of stories who have benefited from G4.

For larger groups of six or more participants, asking everyone to share their story becomes cumbersome. Welcoming guests, which we hope is a regular occurrence, would become an obstacle to the progress of existing group members. In larger groups, invite everyone to share their name and how long they have been a part of the group. Then ask one or two members to share their story. Rotate who you ask so that as new participants are added, everyone has a chance to share and hear each other's stories.

If done well, these introductions are beneficial for both the guest and established members. For your guest, these introductions begin to establish a culture of honesty and a sense that they are not alone in their struggle. For the established members, it is a time to reflect on the collective value of the group. As the group leader, it is wise to verbalize these benefits periodically because they are easy to miss. Drawing attention to beneficial aspects of each part of the group experience is a significant part of your role as a group facilitator.

Stage three: Offer the new participant the opportunity for introduction.

Putting this part of the welcome third allows your guest to ride the momentum of other people's disclosures. Some participants may still prefer to only share their name and limited parts of their story. This is fine. Over time, how much a participant shares becomes a good indicator of their comfort with and commitment to the group.

Regardless of how much a new participant shares, thank them. While sharing our story feels normal to established members, it is new for your guest and, therefore, a mark of courage. As such, it should be affirmed. Appreciation from you as the leader and the group helps create a sense that your guest has made a good choice coming to G4—something that is easy to doubt when we feel vulnerable and uneasy about doing something new.

EXPLAINING COMMITMENT

How many people who realize they need to get in shape, go to a gym, sign up for a membership, but never actually do the work that makes a gym membership valuable? The same dynamic can frequently emerge in counseling groups.

As the group leader, it may feel awkward to talk about commitment. It may feel pushy. But let's continue the example of gym memberships. Is it loving or unloving for a physical trainer to ask "What are your goals for joining our gym? Do you have a sense for what it would take to reach those goals? Can we talk about the things we've noticed in those who join our gym and reach their goals?" While it might be bad for business, these would be loving conversations. Such conversations are what this section is about.

Garnering a commitment to change is a primary focal point of steps 1 and 2 in both the suffering- and sin-based G4 curriculums (we will overview these steps in the next chapter). When a new participant is engaging these early steps, listen not only for what they're learning from the curriculum, but for their level of commitment. The early stages of change are a time when it is easy to turn away because change seems too hard or because they don't like what they would need to acknowledge in order to progress meaningfully.

You can offset these difficulties by inviting an established member to reflect on the early stages of their journey in G4. Perhaps after the new participant shares in a way that indicates their commitment is waning (for example, by displaying flat emotions, expressing discouragement, or saying very little), you can turn to an experienced member of the group and ask, "I remember your work in steps 1 and 2. If I remember correctly, you were frustrated with yourself a good bit. Do you mind sharing with us what that was like for you and when you began to feel more hope?"

Another approach is to verbalize that there is ebb and flow to commitment. You can do this while simultaneously affirming the value of the group: "I know for all of us that our motivation to change can sometimes wane. This is why I am glad we have this group. When my motivation is low, I know you all expect to see me here. When I come, I'm built up by how much you care. Is anyone feeling discouraged right now and in need of a morale boost?"

During the early part of someone's G4 journey, it is wise to check in directly. After group you might pull the new participant aside and ask, "I know you've been here for a few weeks. I appreciate you continuing to come. The early part of change can be hard. How are you doing?" Sometimes a private question can prompt greater honesty with the group. Saying something out loud the first time can break the logjam to talking about it the second, third, and fourth times.

Outside of these early check-in conversations, there are two prompts group leaders can use for conversations about commitment—one positive and one negative. The *positive prompt* is when a participant is doing everything a committed member of the group would do but hasn't verbalized their commitment to the group. In this case, you are merely helping the participant see the value of verbalizing their commitment. The conversation might sound like this:

> "I've noticed you're working hard on your steps. That's encouraging to me as a leader. Thank you. Often when people jump into the process of changing, they can miss the value of verbalizing their commitment. For new participants, sharing can help them see that there is more to G4 than just attending. For established members, it can reinforce that G4 is important and worth committing to. How would you feel about sharing with the group that you value the group and are committed to working your steps until completion?"

Entering the front door (new participants arriving) of G4 requires acknowledging "I *need* help," but closing the back door (participants committing to complete their journey) of G4 involves embracing "I *want* this help." Initially, G4 is a place people must go because things are "that bad." But cultivating commitment transforms G4 into a place people want to go because it's "that helpful." Regularly having participants verbalize this commitment to the group helps create a culture of belonging within your G4 group.

The *negative prompt* is one to use when a participant is sabotaging their own progress and/or disrupting the progress of others. This might include a combination of attending inconsistently, chiding the optimism of fellow group members, glorifying their relapse stories, or repeatedly coming without having done any step work. These actions are different from merely making the social dynamics of the group awkward. We will discuss how to navigate disruptive social dynamics in chapter 16.

When a participant disrupts the ability of other group members to make progress, a private conversation is warranted and might sound something like this:

> "It seems like you may be frustrated. Is that accurate? [Listen and respond to their personal discouragement.] I can understand being discouraged. It's something we all face. Considering what you're feeling, are you still

> committed to seeking to grow through your time at G4?" [Listen.].

Before addressing how this person's actions are affecting the group, it is important to hear where they are personally. The main point is their level of commitment. If they still want to change, you want to help them (without allowing them to disrupt the goals of others). If they no longer want to change, you want to help them acknowledge this and stop pretending (which will only discourage them in the future as they may come to believe that "trying again" wouldn't do any good).

If the participant says they are committed to growing through G4, the next part of the conversation might sound like this:

> "I am glad to hear that. Even when change is hard, it's worth it. Because you're committed to growing through G4, I think it's important for us to discuss how you've impacted the group recently. [Describe.] As a facilitator of the group, I must think for the group as a whole and not only each individual. That means having awkward conversations like this one. If you are committed to the group, you'll be willing to change these things. [Provide examples of how to express their discouragements in ways that do not disrupt the progress of others.] Is that something you are willing to commit to?" [Listen.]

At G4, we are *responsible for* our own change, and we are *committed to* the change of others. This means we conduct ourselves in group in a way that sets others up to flourish. When people are not willing to make this commitment, they are treating G4 like individual counseling. In individual counseling, resistance (although still ineffective) does not disrupt the progress of others, so there is greater margin for resistance in the growth process. In group counseling, each member of the group must honor the other members by conducting themselves in a way that allows everyone to grow.

CONCLUSION

Attendance and commitment are not the same. Part of facilitating a G4 group is helping participants see the value of committing to the process of growth and the well-being of the group. Verbalizing commitment galvanizes the sense of belonging that optimizes the benefits of working on change in a group setting.

Chapter 13

WORKING THE NINE STEPS FOR SIN-BASED STRUGGLES

A core value of G4 is the belief that the gospel speaks to both sin and suffering, but ministers to these experiences differently. For this reason, official G4 curriculum is built around two nine-step models: one for sin-based struggles and one for suffering-based struggles.

In this chapter, we will overview the nine-step model for sin-based struggles; that is, life struggles emerging from our beliefs, values, and choices.[1] We sometimes refer to these steps as the "responsibility model" in order to contrast it with the suffering model, which addresses struggles that do not emerge from a participant's beliefs, values, or choices (to be detailed in the next chapter).

If your G4 group opts to use a non-nine-step curriculum, we will give guidance in chapter 15 for how to effectively use these curriculums in a G4 setting. Even when this is the case, familiarity with these two nine-step models will help you harmonize what

---

1. The content of this chapter is available as a small group study at bradhambrick.com/G4SinModel and can be used for at least two purposes. First, it can be used to raise awareness of G4 within your church by serving as a one-week small group study after your pastor preaches on an emotionally weighty subject like addiction, sexual purity, or anger. Second, it can serve as a good overview tool to familiarize first-time guests with the G4 step work model.

participants are learning in your group with what they learn in large group.

As you go through this chapter, the image we want you to have in mind is a ball bearing. In a ball bearing each of the small inner balls spin to create a smooth rotation for the outer ring. By way of metaphor, each inner ball represents a night at G4, and the outer ring represents the change in an individual's life.

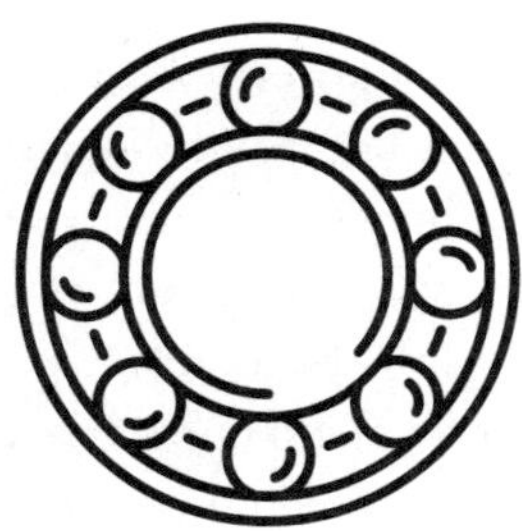

It is common to feel like a given conversation creates more change than has in fact occurred; more is *understood* than *assimilated.* In a conversation, you may feel like your friend has covered the first four steps (i.e., admit, acknowledge, understand, and repent), but when you talk with them next, they have returned to minimizing their sin or blame-shifting.

Progressive sanctification means that there will be rises and falls in our progress. We don't need to be alarmed by the normal process of change. This is another reason why participants may (most often will) spend more than one week on a step. At G4, we are striving to *implement* change, not just *understand* concepts. Implementation is a slower process than mere understanding.

As a rule of thumb, do not gauge progress by where your friend is at the end of a G4 meeting; that is a measure of *understanding* or *desire to change* more than progress. Instead, measure progress based upon where your friend is at the beginning of the next G4 meeting. This represents the difference in movement of the inner balls (i.e., conversation) and the outer ring (i.e., actual change).

With the image of a ball bearing in mind, let's go over the nine G4 steps for change with responsibility-based struggles.

STEP 1: ADMIT I HAVE A STRUGGLE I CANNOT OVERCOME WITHOUT GOD

Admitting we have a life-dominating struggle is something that usually comes and goes (at least at first). This is why someone can reach out for help in a moment of crisis and then get defensive a few days later (maybe even minutes later) when discussing the same life struggle.

The primary goal of step 1 is to garner a consistent commitment to change. If we try to provide practical guidance before someone is committed to change, our best advice—even biblical advice—will be undermined by their inconsistent motivation to change.

Step 1 is also when we realize that we sin because we're sinners, rather than we're sinners because we sin. We are born with an inherent bent toward sin. No one has to teach us to disobey or be selfish. Realizing our sin condition is essential for recognizing the reality that we need more than the removal of a few bad habits. We need a new heart that only Christ can give (Ezekiel 36:26).

STEP 2: ACKNOWLEDGE THE BREADTH AND IMPACT OF MY SIN

You can admit you have an overwhelming struggle and still not acknowledge the breadth and impact of that struggle. Just like you can know that your house needs major repairs and not know the extent or cost of those repairs.

Principle: *Our commitment and effort toward change will be proportional to our belief about the breadth and impact of our struggle.* Imagine a 1 to 10 scale. If you believe you have a size 4 problem, you will give level 4 effort. But if your struggle is size 8, level 4 effort will be inadequate, and you won't make significant progress. Ultimately, not acknowledging the size of the problem will create a defeatist attitude: "I tried. I even tried God's way using the Bible. And it didn't work. What else can be expected of me?"

In step 2 we acknowledge the severity of our sin (its frequency, duration, and magnitude) and our sin's impact on other people (intended or unintended) without wallowing in guilt or shame. During step 2 we acknowledge the futility of making empty promises that change will come quickly.

STEP 3: UNDERSTAND THE ORIGIN, MOTIVE, AND HISTORY OF MY SIN

Too often *acknowledging* (step 2) is confused with *understanding* (step 3). It is as if moments after acknowledging our struggle, we become experts on how to change. We are prone to say with annoyance "I know..." to each insight and practical suggestion we receive. During step 3 we allow God to dissolve this attitude.

A key part of change is humility, and two primary expressions of humility are (a) the willingness to learn and (b) the patience necessary to walk through the learning process. We can say that someone understands their sin when they can discuss the following three things with clarity and without defensiveness:

- *Origin*—How does my struggle reveal the depraved condition of the human race?
- *History*—How has this struggle developed in my life (i.e., family history, personal habits, etc.), and what can I learn from its history?
- *Motive*—What makes this sin appealing to me, and how can I refute the lies implicit in these motives?

Key biblical passages that provide help in step 3 are James 1:14–15 and 4:1–2. In these passages, as Ed Welch explains, we see a transition in the focal point of change from the Old to New Testament.

> The Old Testament theme of idolatry passed the baton to the New Testament themes of lust, cravings, and sinful desire. This is in keeping with the New Testament's emphasis on the hidden commitments of the heart over the external object of our affection. As Scripture unfolds,

> it gradually looks more at our wants and desires and less at the actual idols themselves.[2]

In other words, God is concerned about our behavior because it reveals our heart. We want to help participants see how their behaviors reveal their heart so that they can apply their Bible as God intends.

STEP 4: REPENT TO GOD FOR HOW MY SIN REPLACED AND MISREPRESENTED HIM

Hopefully you are gaining an appreciation for the order of these steps. Repentance is at the heart (i.e., middle) of the change process. However, when our sin hurts others, we are prone to put confession (step 5) at the center of the process. We want making things right with others to be the fuel for change. But expecting forgiveness from people to do what only being right with God can do is ineffective and sets us up to blame others for our continued struggle.

Beyond understanding the order of these steps, a primary task in step 4 is to view repentance as a gift rather than a punishment. Read Romans 2:1–11. While the *fear of the Lord* is the beginning of wisdom (Psalm 111:10; Proverbs 9:10), it is the *kindness of God* that leads us to repentance (Romans 2:4). In step 4 we gain a more accurate understanding of God's demeanor toward us on this journey. Too often we make God in our own image, imagining that he is as frustrated and angry with us as we are with ourselves.

In step 4 we also learn that repentance is about more than feeling sorry in God's presence. Repentance is a wholesale shift in our primary allegiance—from self to God—and a forsaking of the values that made sin seem worth it. The *understanding of idolatrous motives* in step 3 sets us up to do this *repenting of unbiblical values* work in step 4.

2. Ed Welch, *Addictions: A Banquet in the Grave* (Phillipsburg, NJ: P&R, 2001), 203.

STEP 5: CONFESS TO THOSE AFFECTED FOR HARM DONE AND SEEK TO MAKE AMENDS

This is a plumb-line statement of G4: *You will only be as free as you are honest. Privacy kills change and fuels sin. Transparency kills sin and fuels change.* Chances are, this step may scare you as much as any step you've taken since the first one. But remember, it is not nearly as scary to move forward as it is dangerous to drift backward.

Confession serves two functions: (a) acknowledging how we've harmed relationships, seeking forgiveness, and making amends and (b) inviting people to become a more informed part of our support network. Confession is the door to community, the door through which we must pass if we do not want to be alone with our sin. Confession is what invites others into our lives and points out to them where they can help. Confession is how we acknowledge our weakness and admit that we need their help. Confession is what assures others that we have the humility and realistic expectations necessary to be safe to receive help.

STEP 6: RESTRUCTURE MY LIFE TO RELY ON GOD'S GRACE AND WORD TO TRANSFORM MY LIFE

Step 6 is what most people are looking for when they reach out for help. They want practical steps to address their problem. But everything before *life restructuring* creates the context for practical, biblical advice to succeed. These prior steps are summarized in the following list:

- *Admitting* the problem garners motivation and commitment.
- *Acknowledging* the size of the problem removes minimization.
- *Understanding* the motive and history allows practical steps to be more targeted.
- *Repenting* restores relationship with God and removes shame.
- *Confessing* restores key relationships and establishes a support network for change.

Ephesians 4:20–33 provides the basic strategy of step 6: *replacement*. Notice how Paul also calls for replacement as an essential part of change. In verses 20–24, he exhorts his readers not just to "put off" the old but also to "put on" the new, a transformation that is rooted in a profound change in thinking. To illustrate this point, Paul gives examples of change, offering sample replacements for lying (v. 25), anger (vv. 26–27), stealing (v. 28), destructive speech (vv. 29–30), and bitterness (vv. 31–32). In each G4 curriculum, this strategy is individualized for the subject that is being addressed, drawing from the best of Christian and secular literature on that subject.

STEP 7: IMPLEMENT THE NEW STRUCTURE WITH HUMILITY AND FLEXIBILITY

In step 7, we assess the effectiveness of our restructuring plan and make the necessary changes. Temptation does not remain static (Luke 4:13). When we begin to make progress, temptation will change because we have a real enemy bent on our destruction (1 Peter 5:6–11). Therefore, the plan we created in step 6 will need to be updated regularly.

STEP 8: PERSEVERE IN THE NEW LIFE AND IDENTITY TO WHICH GOD HAS CALLED ME

Perseverance is when "better" becomes "normal." When an area of sin becomes life-dominating, the presence of that sin becomes part of the day-to-day normal of our lives. That means holiness feels strange. We must reacclimate to a God-honoring life.

Do a thought experiment. Imagine a mountain in your mind's eye. What do you see? Chances are the image you conjured up was snow-capped peaks. Those snow-capped peaks don't float; something lies beneath them and holds them up.

The same is true for our sin. When we imagine our sin, we see our worst moments. But those worst moments don't float. They sit on top of many lesser compromises that we deemed not that bad.

In the perseverance step (step 8), we begin to root out the "smaller" sins and compromises that upheld the peak sins.

STEP 9: STEWARD ALL OF MY LIFE FOR GOD'S GLORY

To "steward" something means to use it for God's intended purpose. As the law of God is summarized in a positive command in Matthew 22:36–40—something to *do* instead of "thou shall not"—we must always end our battle with sin by talking about how to run to God rather than merely how to run from sin. Life is not about what we avoid, but what we pursue.

To help you assess how to steward your life for God's glory, we offer the following nine questions so that graduation from G4 launches you to live on mission:

1. Am I willing to commit my life to whatever God asks of me?
2. What roles have I neglected that God has placed me in?
3. What are my spiritual gifts?
4. For what group of people am I burdened (age, struggle, career, nation, language, etc.)?
5. What am I passionate about?
6. With what talents or abilities has God blessed me?
7. What are my unique life experiences?
8. Where do my talents and passions match up with the needs in my church and community?
9. How would God have me bring these things together to glorify him?

CONCLUSION

This chapter gives an overview—a generic map of sanctification, the gospel in slow motion for our sin-based struggles. As you lead a G4 group, you will use a curriculum that applies these nine steps to a particular life struggle. But it is important for you to see the big picture and understand how these nine steps build on one another so that as you facilitate your group, you help prevent members from getting lost in the details of anger, addiction, impurity, or other responsibility-based struggles.

In the next chapter, we will turn our attention to the corresponding model for suffering-based struggles.

Chapter 14

WORKING THE NINE STEPS FOR SUFFERING-BASED STRUGGLES

Being a Christian doesn't remove the experience of suffering. Yet, historically, the church's discipleship models for sin-based struggles have been more developed than approaches to suffering-based struggles. It is just clearer to see how the gospel relates to sin—Jesus died for our sin and salvation removes the stain of sin—than it is to see how the gospel addresses suffering. In fact, it can sometimes feel like heaven is God's only remedy for suffering.

That's why this material may seem less intuitive than the previous nine-step model. But it also explains why this material is so needed. In a broken world, we will suffer in many ways. We need to understand how to minister the gospel to people who are suffering.

The nine-step model for suffering is both *sequential* (i.e., in steps) and *segmented* (i.e., those steps cluster together to create three stages of change). It will help orient you to this model if you keep these stages in mind:

- **Stage one:** Stabilize and understand the experience of suffering (steps 1 through 3)
- **Stage two:** Identify and correct the narrative scripts that arise from suffering (steps 4 through 6)

- **Stage three:** Engage healthily with life and relationships after suffering (steps 7 through 9)

Like we did in the previous chapter, we will explore generically what each G4 suffering-based curriculum (grief, trauma, depression, betrayal, etc.) covers with greater specificity.[1] The goal of this chapter is to give you the big picture and to help you understand the progression from one step to the next.

STEP 1: PREPARE YOURSELF PHYSICALLY, EMOTIONALLY, AND SPIRITUALLY TO FACE YOUR SUFFERING

When suffering has been long and hard, we feel exhausted in every way possible. Reaching out for help is an act of courage and should be honored as such. Just as the widow's mite was celebrated by Jesus because it was a gift from *financial poverty* (Luke 21:1–4), we want to honor asking for help as an act of faith expressed out of *hope poverty*.

Step 1 examines some relatively mundane parts of our life: sleep, eating habits, exercise, social support, and prioritizing key decisions. Responding well to suffering requires endurance, and these mundane parts of life either aid or undermine our endurance. In step 1, we honor the reality that we are embodied souls living in a world of high demands by thinking through how to care for our bodies and respond to these demands in a way that sets us up to complete this journey well.

STEP 2: ACKNOWLEDGE THE SPECIFIC HISTORY AND REALNESS OF MY SUFFERING

As we are using the term, *acknowledging* means looking at the facts and calling things by the right name. There are many barriers that

1. The content of this chapter is available as a small group study at bradhambrick.com/G4SufferingModel and can be used for at least two purposes. First, it can be used to raise awareness of G4 within your church by serving as a one-week small group study after your pastor preaches on an emotionally weighty subject like trauma, betrayal, or grief. Second, it can serve first-time guests at G4 as a good overview to familiarize them with the G4 step work model.

may prevent us from acknowledging our suffering—barriers like shame, shock, past or present threats, lies from an abuser, confusion because of the age at which suffering occurred, loyalty, or denial as part of grief.

Different types of suffering create unique challenges to acknowledging the realness of our experience. Adultery is clouded with lies. Trauma is fragmented. Abuse involves blame-shifting. Grief is surreal. We can often start to feel crazy because of how our perspective fluctuates about what happened.

We will only make good application of the Bible when we rightly understand our experience. That's why in suffering the first step toward change is not asking "What does the Bible say?" but "What am I experiencing?" If we are wrong about the second question (assessing our experience), we won't make good use of answers to the first question (Bible interpretation).

It is important to realize that as we talk about these "facts and events" we are recalling them from within a story (step 4). But that narrative is the only way we know how to tell what happened. Realizing that the narrative we use to understand these events may not be accurate is scary and unsettling. But it is an important part of responding in wiser, healthier ways.

STEP 3: UNDERSTAND THE IMPACT OF MY SUFFERING

Between facts (step 2) and story (step 4) is impact (step 3). Things happen, they make an impact, and then we make sense of that impact with a narrative. Use the following vignette of how a child narrates the experience of abuse to understand the relationship of steps two and three. We'll consider this vignette again in step 4.

- **Step 2:** Facts—Bad things happened.
  - » Parent hits child because a toy was out of place.
  - » Painful words were spoken, and the other parent leaves the room.
  - » Child cries without comfort.
  - » People slowly return, and life becomes "normal" again.
  - » Wait for next explosion.

- **Step 3:** Impact—Suffering changes how we understand and respond to life.
  - » Authority figures are viewed as unapproachable or dangerous.
  - » Pain is viewed as something to be endured alone.
  - » Pain is viewed as something that intrudes without reason or warning.
  - » See others living "normal" lives and experience confusion, anger, or jealousy.
  - » Every mistake, or potential mistake, carries the emotional weight of great pain.

Notice how the events—the facts of the abuse—are more than just painful memories. They have a broad, ongoing impact on the person who experienced them.

Some people will look at the bullet points above and think, *My suffering wasn't that bad because others have suffered much worse than me.* But *suffering is not a competitive sport.*[2] Recovering from knee surgery doesn't hurt less because someone else got hit by a truck. To interpret suffering rightly, we need to assess our suffering on its own terms, not comparing it to others' suffering.

STEP 4: LEARN MY SUFFERING STORY THAT I USE TO MAKE SENSE OF MY EXPERIENCE

In this step, we articulate the destructive messages (you might call them stories, narrative, or scripts) we take from the facts (step 2) and impact (step 3) of our suffering to try to make sense of these painful experiences. To illustrate this, let's return to the example of an abused child and consider the kinds of suffering stories this child might take from their experience of abuse.

- **Step 4:** Story—We make sense of suffering in destructive ways
  - » "I am a person who doesn't deserve to be protected."

---

2. If you struggle with this mentality, consider reading the article "Making Peace with Romans 8:28," which can be found at bradhambrick.com/romans828.

» "I am living in a world that only plays by the rules for other people."
» "Love is a cruel joke that you can't live without but blows up in your face when you get it."

We may theologically disagree with most everything we say on this step. But there is still value in putting these destructive scripts into words. Just because how we make sense of our suffering isn't *true* doesn't mean the effect of that narrative isn't *real*. In order to move our narrative toward truth, we must grapple with how we actually think.

Let's take the example of a child who is afraid to learn to swim. The child's fear is a *real* experience. They have an increased heart rate, pupil dilation, and a change in breathing pattern. But the story behind the fear—"I'm going to drown"—is *false*. However, it does a parent no good to try to truth bomb the child out of their fear—"If I were going to drown you, would I do it in front of this many people?" Instead, empathy toward the real experience—"This feels like a big deal, doesn't it?"—builds trust so that the distortions in how the child is telling their story can be addressed—"You're a strong kid who is good at learning new things."

The Psalms often take this approach to untying the knots in how we make sense of suffering. The Psalms are unique in Scripture because they are a place where God gives us words to speak back to him during our best and worst times. Of particular comfort during times of suffering is the fact that God sometimes puts "heresy" in the Psalms. God allowed untrue statements to be included in the Psalms because they capture our experience of living mid-journey in a broken world.

- God is felt to be hiding from us in our troubles (Psalm 10:1)
- God is felt to be forgetful or uninterested in our suffering (Psalm 13:1; 44:24)
- God is felt to have forsaken those who cry out to him (Psalm 22:1–2)
- God is felt to be asleep and therefore unaware (Psalm 44:23)

- God is felt to have abandoned his people forever (Psalm 74:1)
- God is felt to have aggressively "spiked" an innocent person in anger (Psalm 102:10)

God is not agreeing with these false interpretations, but he is demonstrating his willingness to be compassionate toward the realness of our experience before he tries to correct our interpretation of what is true. God wants to transform our suffering story, but he is willing to enter it where we are and patiently transform our story from within.

STEP 5: MOURN THE WRONGNESS OF WHAT HAPPENED AND RECEIVE GOD'S COMFORT

Many of us probably feel like this step is out of place. After we articulate destructive thinking, we want to replace it with helpful thinking as soon as possible. Also, because we tend to think that mourning happens either at the beginning or end of a movie, not the middle, it seems odd for this to be a central step in our nine-step, suffering journey.

Mourning signifies a time of transition. We mourn at the major pivots of our life (good and bad). We cry at weddings and funerals because we recognize the profound transition that is taking place. In these nine steps, we are at a point of transition. This is the first time we can look at what really happened (step 2) and understand its impact (step 3) without embracing the destructive messages that were embedded with our suffering (step 4). We can finally "grieve clean."

Notice that Paul offers his famous "weep with those who weep" advice in the passage on how to respond to suffering (Romans 12:14–21). *Paul did not try to meet suffering with an answer, but instead with empathy*. When we have removed the destructive messages from our suffering, we are able to receive compassion from God (Matthew 5:4) and friends without it feeling like they are validating those destructive themes.

STEP 6: LEARN MY GOSPEL STORY BY WHICH GOD GIVES MEANING TO MY EXPERIENCE

Suffering does not get the final word on our life. *Mourning* is when we allow God to affirm that our suffering is real and that we matter to him. But compassion is not all that God has to offer.

God wants to help us make sense of our suffering through the grand redemptive narrative of the gospel, to the degree that we can before we experience the full redemption of all things in heaven. However, the segmented way we are prone to read our Bibles can impede God's intent. In *The Drama of Scripture: Finding Our Place in the Biblical Story,* Craig Bartholomew and Michael Goheen write,

> Many of us have read the Bible as if it were merely a mosaic of little bits—theological bits, moral bits, historical-critical bits, sermon bits, devotional bits. But when we read the Bible in such a fragmented way, we ignore its divine author's intention to shape our lives through its story. All human communities live out of some story that provides a context for understanding the meaning of history and gives shape and direction to their lives. If we allow the Bible to become fragmented, it is in danger of being absorbed into whatever other story is shaping our culture, and it will thus cease to shape our lives as it should. . . . If, as believers, we allow this story (rather than the Bible) to become the foundation of our thought and action, then our lives will manifest not the truths of Scripture, but the lies of an idolatrous culture.[3]

Looking to the Bible's story as we process our suffering doesn't mean that we get an answer to the why question we've asked so many times. It *does* mean we begin to answer the big questions of life in meaningful and satisfying ways in light of all that God has done in response to sin and the fall. These questions might include:

---

3. Craig Bartholomew and Michael Goheen, *The Drama of Scripture: Finding Our Place in the Biblical Story* (Grand Rapids, MI: Baker Academic, 2014), 12.

Who am I now? Who is God, and where is he amid my suffering? What parts of this hardship am I responsible for, and what parts are "just suffering"? How should I think about the people who hurt me? Is love worth grief? What is worth living for in light of what I've been through?

STEP 7: IDENTIFY GOALS THAT ALLOW ME TO COMBAT THE IMPACT OF MY SUFFERING

Some of us resist calling our hardship suffering because we think this means accepting there is nothing we can do about it. Just because something is not our fault doesn't mean we are powerless to fight the consequences of what happened. Acknowledging suffering does not mean we have to be passive. We can actively work to offset the impact of our suffering without accepting responsibility for the original hardship(s).

In this sense, step 7 is the mirror of step 3. In step 3, we gained an understanding of how suffering impacted our life. After step 3, we took an intermission to ensure that we were not making sense of our suffering in destructive ways (step 4 through step 6). Now, in step 7, we begin to do the work of offsetting the impact of our suffering.

Again, suffering comes in many forms, and each form can have a unique impact. The relational impact of betrayal is different from the physical impact of chronic pain, and the emotional impact of trauma is different still. Step 7 is when each G4 curriculum draws upon the best of Christian and clinical literature on that subject to offer subject-specific strategies to offset the impact of that type of suffering.

STEP 8: PERSEVERE IN THE NEW LIFE AND IDENTITY TO WHICH GOD HAS CALLED ME

Perseverance makes "better" become "normal." When an aspect of suffering becomes life-dominating, the impact of suffering becomes part of the day-to-day normal of our lives. That means healthy emotions and relationships feel strange. We must reacclimate to the kind of life God wants for us.

While we acclimate to a healthy normal, we may experience anger, regret, or guilt as we begin to see the past for what it could have been. These emotions are unpleasant, but not bad. They are another opportunity to mourn (step 5). And they mean that this is an important time to continue the process of understanding our personal story as a part of God's larger story of redemption.

STEP 9: STEWARD ALL OF MY LIFE FOR GOD'S GLORY

To "steward" something means to use it for God's intended purpose. As the law of God is summarized in a positive command in Matthew 22:36–40—something to *do* instead of a "thou shall not"—then we must always end our battle against suffering by finding ways to run to God rather than merely how to run from the effects of suffering. Life is not about what we avoid, but what we pursue.

To help you assess how to steward your life for God's glory, we offer the following nine questions so that graduation from G4 launches you to live on mission:

1. Am I willing to commit my life to whatever God asks of me?
2. What roles have I neglected that God has placed me in?
3. What are my spiritual gifts?
4. For what group of people am I burdened (age, struggle, career, nation, language, etc.)?
5. What am I passionate about?
6. With what talents or abilities has God blessed me?
7. What are my unique life experiences?
8. Where do my talents and passions match up with the needs in my church and community?
9. How would God have me bring these things together to glorify him?

CONCLUSION

This chapter provides an overview. We drew a generic map for enduring and responding to suffering well. As you lead a G4 group, you will use a curriculum that applies these nine steps to a particular life struggle. But it is important for you to see the big picture and understand how these steps build on one another so that as you facilitate your group, you can help members not to get lost in the details of grief, trauma, betrayal, or other suffering-based struggles.

Now that we have overviewed each of the G4 nine-step models, we will turn our attention to how to utilize curriculum that is not built around these nine-step models. God has blessed the church with other resources, using other outlines, and we designed G4 to help your church have a context for utilizing those resources effectively.

Chapter 15

USING A NON-NINE-STEP CURRICULUM WITHOUT CONFUSION

This chapter is only relevant if you have a ministry of multiple groups. If you have a single group that doesn't use a G4 curriculum, for instance a DivorceCare group, there is no confusion about it not using a nine-step curriculum. It isn't called G4. No one is confused, so there is no need for clarification.

But once you have a collection of groups called a G4 ministry at your church, confusion may arise when some groups use nine-step curriculums and others do not; some curriculums have the G4 logo, while others don't. This is not a problem to be fixed, but instead a point of confusion to be clarified.

AN INTENTIONAL PROBLEM

From its inception, G4 was designed to utilize curriculums from other authors that were written in other formats. We knew our G4 curriculum would not be the only effective or helpful curriculum a church might use. We also recognized that these other counseling curriculums didn't fit naturally in a church's discipleship system. That's the reason we wanted to create a ministry infrastructure to help churches use other group counseling curriculums well.

Hopefully you are beginning to see that G4 is more than a series of curriculums. It is a ministry model that allows your church to utilize a variety of counseling curriculums effectively. Think of it like a Coca-Cola machine. Yes, it is a place to get a can of Coke. But it is also a place to get other soft drinks as well. Yes, G4 uses G4 curriculums, but it is also a place that allows your church to utilize other good counseling curriculums.

That raises the question "What constitutes a *good* curriculum?" We won't answer that question for you. We believe each church should decide what best fits their theology and needs. The seven core values of G4 (chapter 4) should guide your assessment. We know every church won't agree theologically or therapeutically about each curriculum they use in their G4 ministry. We're okay with that.

If you would like a list of some curriculums that fit within a G4 structure, we keep an updated list at bradhambrick.com/G4curriculum. Simply take this list for what it is—a prompt for your church to brainstorm possibilities.

HOW DO WE USE OTHER CURRICULUMS?

Let's approach this question by tracing the steps of a group participant to determine when confusion might arise. First, a person hears about your church's G4 ministry and learns—probably from the church's website—that there is a group that matches their need. No confusion yet; just excitement.

Next, the guest arrives at the designated time and location. After being greeted, they enter the large group time. If you've thought through your welcoming strategy, there is still no confusion, though there may be a bit of nervousness.

During large group, they hear a brief overview of one of the seven core values or one of the nine steps. Even at this point, we don't have confusion. But we have created an expectation that may lead to confusion. If a participant doesn't find nine steps in their subject-specific group, their brow may furrow. Four steps will remedy that potential confusion.

First, regardless of which curriculum they are using, every leader in a G4 ministry should be familiar with the nine steps for both responsibility-based and suffering-based struggles. Reading chapters 13 and 14, especially as these steps are reviewed weekly in large group, should provide adequate familiarity with these two models.

Second, when using a non-nine-step curriculum, the G4 director and G4 group facilitator should discuss whether sin or suffering is more at the forefront in that group. For instance, if you use Steven Tracy's *Mending the Soul* curriculum[1] on recovering from domestic abuse, suffering would be at the forefront. But if you use Chris Moles's *Men of Peace* curriculum[2] for abusers, sin would be at the forefront. A curriculum like CCEF's *Uncovering Guilt and Shame*[3] would be a strong mix between the two nine-step models.

Third, you should read through the non-nine-step curriculum and note where that book addresses the primary themes of the nine steps for sin or suffering. When you see a theme from one of the nine steps, write that number in the margin. A good Christian resource will address these nine themes, even if it does not use the same language. As you discuss your curriculum in group, you want to be able to say, "What we're working through here corresponds with step number (add the number) in the nine-step models we hear about in large group."

Fourth, work through your curriculum with your group as designed by its author without further alteration or commentary. No more clarification is needed. The curriculum for the group should be in the foreground. Periodic orientations to the G4 nine-step models allow group members to place the work they're doing within the sanctification paradigms presented in large group.

---

1. Steven R. Tracy, *Mending the Soul: Understanding and Healing Abuse* (Grand Rapids, MI: Zondervan, 2008).
2. Chris Moles, *Men of Peace*, self-paced course, https://chrismoles.podia.com/men-of-peace-coaching-course-coach-s-copy.
3. David Powlison, Ed Welch, Joe Novenson, *Uncovering Guilt and Shame*, video curriculum (CCEF), https://www.ccef.org/curriculum/uncovering-shame-guilt-curriculum/.

With these steps in place, leading a non-nine-step group should not feel different from using that material in another setting. The infrastructure of G4 allows for the church to know when and where to utilize such a curriculum and how to differentiate it from material used in a general discipleship group, as well as providing support for the group leader who would be more prone to burnout if the group were led in isolation.

Following these steps should allow your G4 ministry to use any group-based curriculum that your church affirms and which meets a need in your community. As you use other curriculums, we want you to know you are fulfilling a design element that was intentionally embedded in G4 from the beginning. Thank you for allowing the work of these other authors to minister to people in your community. We are elated that G4 can help you do this!

Chapter 16

WORKING WITH "THAT" PARTICIPANT

If you expect some relational difficulties in your group, you won't be surprised when they occur. But this expectation doesn't have to be rooted in cynicism. Difficult moments in group can be some of the most fruitful times. After all, learning to navigate difficulty is the reason people come to G4.

Principle: *the difficulties emerging in group usually mirror the difficulties that brought that person to group*. That is what makes these moments ripe for change.

In this chapter we will consider five dynamics that often get someone labeled as "that participant" and discuss how to respond in constructive ways. Are these approaches fail proof? No. But even if they are less effective at curbing the disruptive behavior than you would like, these approaches will result in the other group members learning to respond to difficult moments better. And that's your role as a group facilitator—to use each part of the group experience to facilitate the opportunity for growth for everyone present.

1. NON-PARTICIPATION

Yes, a non-participating participant is a contradiction in terms. But just because it is an oxymoron (like the phrases "jumbo shrimp," "only choice," or "awfully good") does not mean it won't appear.

It is common for first time participants to be reticent to share. Don't rush them. That's not who we're talking about here. We're talking about the person who persistently doesn't engage with the group, even after attending for some time.

Why is it important to address non-participation? Distrust emerges when the level of vulnerability in the group is imbalanced. Each person sharing is a key part of what makes a G4 group feel safe. There is a sense that *we* know each other and are working toward a common goal. However, someone perpetually present but silent creates a "why are *you* here" sense. This can result in the development of an insider versus outsider dynamic that causes those who are sharing to feel watched.

Strategy: Initially, assume that silence is motivated by fear rather than resistance. Before or after group, look for an opportunity for a one-on-one conversation and ask about their comfort level in group and hesitancy to share. If possible, adjust the group to provide safe ways for the participant to engage in group. You can also ask what they would share in group if they were more comfortable. Sharing with you first can serve as a practice run for sharing with the group. Ask their permission to prompt them to share with the group what they shared with you.

2. MONOPOLIZING

If some participants won't step up to the mic, other participants never surrender the mic (metaphorically speaking). They may talk for too long, give too many details, seem to have no perceivable purpose for their stories, or control conversations by hijacking any topic, forcing it back to their experiences or concerns.

What is going on here? These participants are treating *group counseling* as if it were *individual counseling*. Individual counseling is all about you and your change. Group counseling is not. Group counseling is about learning to change alongside others. The skill of being other-minded while working on personal growth may be one of the more important social skills that participants learn in group counseling. It is one of the things that makes G4 special.

Strategy: Initially, assume that overspeaking is motivated by a lack of self-awareness, rather than selfishness. Periodically, it is wise to remind the group of the duration for disclosures that ensure everyone can participate. Calling first on a group member who understands the appropriate length of disclosure can help serve as an example and establish a rhythm for the evening. If this is ineffective, address the individual directly but gently, privately first. Discuss the impact of the length of their disclosures on the group. Coach them on how to concisely share parts of their story or progress on one of the nine steps. Advise that they give forethought to what they would like to share, with consideration to sharing what is most important in a timely manner.

3. CONFLICT

Times of change are times of conflict. G4 is a place of change. That means as you facilitate a G4 group, you will inevitably navigate conflict. We will discuss the normalcy of conflict in the life cycle of a group again in section three.

Conflicts may arise between group members or between a member and a leader, or a conflict that exists outside of the group may be discussed in group. While conflict can cause some participants to feel uncomfortable, navigating conflict around needed areas of change is another life skill learned through group counseling.

Strategy: Initially, assume the conflict mirrors challenges the participant(s) also need(s) to learn to navigate outside of group. For instance, a participant who struggles with defensiveness when acknowledging failures outside of group will likely also be defensive when acknowledging setbacks in group. The here and now of group life mirrors the then and there of home life. This helps you identify the in-group value for engaging how the conflict is expressed.

Guiding the group through the process of learning to explore options and considering other perspectives is a way to reverse the constrictive style of thinking that naturally emerges during conflict.

Whether or not the specific conflict is satisfactorily resolved, this approach ensures that everyone in group is practicing a valuable life skill during these uncomfortable discussions. By constructively engaging conflict, you will also gain respect as a leader of the group.

4. BLAME-SHIFTING

Blame-shifting is when we blame someone else for a problem of our own making. In effect, we are responding to our *sin* as if it were *suffering*. Learning to differentiate sin and suffering is a primary task in G4. Instances of blame-shifting are times when we get to review these foundational concepts.

We can all relate to the temptation toward blame-shifting. It is a form of wishful thinking: "I wish you had done [blank] because I would have been less prone to [blank]." Even when this sentence is true—we may have been less prone toward a problematic response—this style of thinking remains problematic. Blame-shifting reveals a drift toward a sense of powerlessness, believing that our choices are not the most influential factor in our life.

Strategy: We should approach blame-shifting with sympathetic disagreement. Sympathetic because there is a legitimate hardship. Disagreement because owning what we can control is essential to change. Creating a group culture where people focus on how their choices can influence their life is essential to this sympathetic disagreement not feeling personal. If this is what "we" are all striving to do (i.e., resist blame-shifting), then it's less personal to discuss "your" response in this moment.

5. LACK OF COMMITMENT

Groups have collective momentum, and low-commitment members serve as a speed bump for the group's momentum. It would be easy to merely appeal to a low-commitment group member by stating, "We want a better outcome for you." That is true, but it's not the whole truth. We are also protecting the growth of other group members.

Because there must be commitment for any significant change to occur, we stress it from the moment a new participant joins our group (see chapter 12). The importance of commitment should be discussed frequently, not just when there is a problem. Here we are discussing when the commitment level of previously engaged group members begins to wane. The fact that these individuals have an established relationship with you and the group means that their waning commitment hurts the group more. But it also means you should have more history and relational capital to draw from as you address the issue.

Strategy: Start with a compassionate statement like, "You have not seemed like yourself in recent weeks. Is something bothering you?" When you discuss the impact of their dip in commitment on the group, frame it as an indication of how much the group cares for them. For example, "Because you've been here for a while and people respect you, your demeanor has a larger than average impact." If the struggle persists, invite them to acknowledge and share the reason for their decline in motivation with the group. Honesty and vulnerability about the struggle offset the impact on the group's collective momentum.

CONCLUSION

You are now commissioned to serve as the VP of Navigating Awkward Situations for your group. That is the unwritten subtitle to your official title, G4 facilitator. Think of leading a G4 group like being Gandalf in *The Lord of the Rings*; your work is to facilitate the journey and maintain harmony within the fellowship.

Fortunately, you don't have to be a sage wizard to accomplish these tasks. You do need to be willing to walk toward difficult moments with a compassionate smile, to articulate the good opportunities a disruption reveals, and have the courage to talk through the implications. This chapter has foreshadowed the most common challenges so that you can think through in advance how to respond effectively.

Section Three: *Facilitating* the Life Cycle of a Group

As a G4 facilitator, you are *leading the group* more than you are *leading the individuals* within that group. This distinction can be difficult to grasp at first. For that reason, we will spend section three tracing the life cycle of the group—treating the group as its own organism. Our goal is twofold. First, we want to help you understand and know how to navigate common group dynamics. To that end, we'll take an in-depth look at the five stages in the life of a group. Second, we want to further reinforce the mentality that you are the leader of a group experience rather than the counselor for six to twelve individuals sitting in a circle.

Chapter 17

G4 AS AN OPEN GROUP MODEL

There are different types of groups, not just different subjects that can be addressed in groups. It is easy to only think of the topics that might receive care at G4—experiences like addiction, depression, or trauma. But thinking this way will make our preparation incomplete.

In this chapter, we will consider three ways to differentiate types of groups before focusing primarily on the third distinction as an introduction to the life cycles of a group.

DIFFERENCES IN COUNSELING GROUPS

First, counseling groups can be professional or peer-based. Professional counseling groups are led by a credentialed counselor. Participants pay to be a part of these groups. The counselor has expertise in the subject matter being discussed. As a lay-based ministry, G4 groups are peer-based, meaning the leader is a nonprofessional facilitating a curriculum while drawing upon their personal experience with the struggle.

If your community has professional groups available, don't view them as competitors, even if the subject matter overlaps. There is enough brokenness in our world that we don't have to compete over souls to care for. If you do a good job in G4, it is likely these professionals will consider your group as aftercare for their participants or a referral option for those who cannot afford their group.

Second, counseling groups can have different styles or purposes for interaction. As we explained in chapter 3, the 4 in G4 represents the number of groups that can be housed within the G4 counseling ministry: (a) recovery groups, for dealing with destructive life patterns; (b) process groups, to reduce the life disruption from difficult experiences in the past; (c) support groups, to encourage participants as they walk through hard times; and (d) therapeutic educational groups, to help participants better understand their life challenges.

In a peer-based setting like G4, each group will emphasize one of these styles more than the others. While every group will embody the seven core values of G4 (chapter 4), groups may vary in their atmosphere based on which type of curriculum that group is utilizing.

Third, counseling groups can be open or closed. Open groups have new participants joining at any time, while closed groups have a short window of time early in the life of the group when new participants can join. G4 may have either open or closed groups, but most groups will be open. We focus on this distinction because it has the greatest impact on how your group will progress through the five stages of group life that we'll walk through in the next chapters. These stages are:

- Stage one: Creating a sense of "us" (chapter 18)
- Stage two: Navigating resistance to change (chapter 19)
- Stage three: Creating a shared culture (chapter 20)
- Stage four: Doing the hard work of change (chapter 21)
- Stage five: Graduating and celebrating friends (chapter 22)

All groups—whether professional or peer-based, whether they are focused on recovery, support, processing, or therapeutic education—will go through these five stages. Whether a group is open or closed will determine *how* a group progresses through these stages.

We will discuss closed groups first, even though they are less prevalent in G4, because the progression through these stages is simpler in closed groups than in open groups.

CLOSED GROUPS

In a closed group, all participants start and finish at basically the same time. Closed groups tend to be groups with a set duration. For instance, many curriculums written for churches are designed to be thirteen-week experiences. After the first couple of weeks in a closed group, too much ground has been covered for new members to effectively join the group.

If a thirteen-week closed group begins in early January and a would-be participant asks to join that group in mid-February, it will be too late to join the current group, and the person would likely need to wait until at least May before a new group begins. Narrow entry points make it more difficult to communicate with your church and surrounding community about when groups are available. Knowing someone can always join a group is vital for pastors, church members, and community leaders to effectively recommend a ministry like G4.

But to understand the life cycle of a group, closed groups are clear. Everyone begins with limited or no connection to each other and must work to create a sense of belonging within the group (stage one). As greater vulnerability emerges, members realize there is now no reason not to be more honest (stage two). After that, members acclimate to the social norms and expectations of this new group (stage three). With greater authenticity, fruitful change materializes consistently in the life of group members (stage four). Then, those who complete their journey are affirmed and celebrated (stage five).

When everyone starts and finishes at the same time, the stages are encountered in order—one-two-three-four-five. Further, because everyone is working on the same content at the same time, the progress through these five stages is highly (but not completely) synchronized. For these reasons, closed groups have predictable life cycles. Without the influx of new participants to alter the life cycle, only serious unforeseen circumstances disrupt the progression.

OPEN GROUPS

By contrast, open groups are perpetually accessible to new participants. People can join at any time. Because every participant is working through the same set of steps, each participant may be at a different point on their journey.

When an open group launches, the life cycle initially feels like a closed group because everyone starts at the same time. But in the middle stages, compared to a closed group, the open group's development will begin to "lag behind" as it assimilates new members. (Here "lag behind" is in quotation marks because this phenomenon is not as negative as the phrase suggests).

In an established open group, all five group stages may be happening at the same time. As the initial members of a group are acclimating to the group culture (stage three) and doing the work of change (stage four), new guests are cultivating a sense of belonging (stage one) and navigating their resistance to being vulnerable (stage two). Later, these same things will continue, while the group is also graduating people who are completing their journey (stage five).

When participants are at different stages in how they relate to the group, you as the leader will need to be alert and assist the group in navigating the tensions arising from those differences. To illustrate, if an established group of five members (perhaps settled in at stage four) gets an influx of four new participants, the group may feel like it has regressed. The "norms" are no longer normal. Unless these differences are verbalized and addressed well, established members will feel like new participants are an interruption and new participants will feel like established members are cliquish.

In the following chapters, we will help you facilitate these asynchronous journeys and shepherd your group through these stages together. For now, it is enough to see and understand these dynamics of ebb and flow. It is okay to feel a little overwhelmed and seasick. Leading an open group feels more like riding an ocean liner over uneven seas than the steady, rhythmic bumps of traveling by train.

But leading an open group is worth it for at least the following three reasons:

1. Open groups are *more effective for outreach*.
2. Open groups are *authentic to real life*.
3. Open groups are *holistic*, allowing simultaneous insight from the entire change process.

Often, in church, we think **outreach** only means evangelism. Here we are using outreach to mean "the ability to impact our desired audience," who may be believers or unbelievers. When groups have narrow entry points, it limits their availability for their desired audience. From our example of thirteen-week curriculums, there would be eight weeks per year when someone can join a group, instead of fifty-two. That is the reason most groups in your G4 ministry should strive to be open groups, unless the advantages of a closed group for a given subject or curriculum are significant.

In **real life**, challenges do not patiently align themselves with where we are in our growth process. Education is linear; it provides initial concepts before more advanced concepts. That is great as you move from addition and subtraction to multiplication and division to algebraic equations. Schools arrange tests to align with this progression. But in real life, change is not linear; challenges come in whatever order they happen to come. Having a G4 group where there is a structured journey (step work models) with people at different points on their journeys provides the benefit of both structure and real life fluidity.

Finally, regularly hearing from people at every point on the journey allows for a **holistic** approach. New participants get to hear the wisdom and warnings of people further along on their journey. Established members get the humility and encouragement that comes with being reminded of where they started. A sense of family emerges as each G4 group begins to have "generations" within it.

Does this mean open groups yield all benefit and no challenges? Clearly, no. As the group facilitator, you will notice and feel the challenges of leading an open group. As with anything in group, be honest about it. Honesty and authenticity are the lifeblood of growth and change. But keep these three points in mind to remind your group why the challenges are worth it.

Chapter 18

STAGE ONE: CREATING A SENSE OF "US"

Everything that's alive develops. Only inanimate objects remain the same. You want your G4 group to be a place of life, so you should expect it to go through a developmental process. Your group should grow and, if it grows, it will experience growing pains. In this chapter, we are going to explore the first stage of your group's developmental process, when a collection of strangers come together with a common struggle and become a group of allies striving together toward a common goal.[1]

WHERE AM I? DO I BELONG HERE?

These are the two primary questions a new participant asks during stage one, whether they can articulate these questions or not. Because your participants are finding their feet, you, as the leader, will be more directive and didactic (i.e., teaching) during this stage of development than in other stages. To progress from a collection of people in a circle to a cohesive group requires someone to share

---

1. This book is written at a lay level for leaders of peer-based (i.e., nonprofessional) groups. If you want a graduate school treatment of the developmental process of counseling groups, consider *The Theory and Practice of Group Psychotherapy*, 6th ed. by Irvin D. Yalom (New York, NY: Basic Books, 2020). There you will find a more in-depth examination of these five stages from a secular (but not anti-Christian) perspective.

the purpose and expectations of the group. That person is you as a G4 facilitator.

Imagine yourself as a first-time guest to G4. You're not sure your struggle is "that bad." There is a social awkwardness because you don't know the other people or how the group will be run. You simultaneously feel *pressure, uncertainty, and loneliness* (i.e., a lack of belonging). The goal of stage one is to remove these emotional and relational obstacles.

You do this by clarifying simple things such as

- Names—Who are the other people here?
- Rhythms—How does this group operate?
- Expectations—What, how much, and when do I have to share here?
- Confidentiality—What happens with what I share here?
- Culmination—How do I know when I'm done?

It is easy to forget what you didn't know when you started in G4. These things were once points of angst for you as well.

You want to answer these questions in a succinct and conversational way that invites questions. You want to use normal words, phrases, and cadence because that helps G4 feel authentic. You want to be concise because long explanations communicate complexity and that participants are here to listen. You want to invite questions because early questions foster sharing later in the group experience.

In stage one of your group's development, you are building on the welcome material that we covered in chapters 7 and 12. Now is a good time to review that material.

To help a new participant develop a sense of belonging, you might welcome them this way:

> "I'm glad you're here. [smile] There are several things people usually want to know when they come to G4. I'm happy to answer those questions and any others you might have. G4 is a place we come because we want to grow.

> We're willing to own our faults and challenges so that we can overcome them.
>
> In group, we are each working through the nine steps at our own pace,[2] which means each of us is at a different place in our journey. At G4, no one gets rushed, and no one gets left behind. We use group time to update each other about where we are on our journey, to learn more about what change requires, and to encourage one another. As a guest, you are welcome to share as much or as little of your story as you feel comfortable sharing.
>
> Once you commit to the group, if you choose to do so, there are two primary things we expect of one another: being honest and honoring the honesty of others. Being honest means admitting when we fall so that we can fall forward. Honoring the honesty of others means we don't talk about anyone else's story outside of group. Each person is in charge of who knows their story.
>
> There's no set time commitment for finishing the steps. Folks stay until they've done what they came to do, and we celebrate with them when it's done.
>
> If that overview sounds appealing, I'd love to have you be a part of our group. [smile] What can I clarify for you?" [Listen.]

Obviously, you will need to put this vignette into your own words and cadence. But this sample gives you the essence of what you're communicating to new guests. Take a moment and write a version of this introduction in your words. Read what you wrote out loud to hear yourself say it. Put the paper down and practice saying it without notes.

---

2. If your group is using a non-nine-step curriculum you would adapt this part of the sample monologue.

WHAT DOES IT LOOK LIKE WHEN A NEW GROUP IS STARTING?

When a group is starting, you are the group. You are the only person that anyone is confident will be back next week. This means you will speak in the first person singular more (i.e., I, me, my). This chapter is all about facilitating the "I to we" transition.

You'll know you've made the "I to we" transition when you hear the echo of other group members saying, "Yeah, my name is [blank] and I agree. We're glad you're here." As this happens, you can add to your opening vignette, "In tonight's group we have people who have been here for up to [blank] months, and we're all excited to continue our journey with you as part of the group."

Read through the monologue again. This time consider the emotions you are helping your guest assuage. Early instruction about the group is more about settling someone's emotions than teaching things to remember. Until someone is comfortable, they probably won't remember much of what you say. Further, they may not understand much of what you initially share with them until they see, experience, and do it. Explaining G4 is like describing the sweet tartness of a strawberry. Even when the words make sense, you don't "get it" until you take a bite. Your words in these stage one conversations are about helping your guest emotionally settle into the notion that G4 is a safe place to talk about hard things and a place where many people have found hope.

For this reason, during stage one, posture and tone accomplish more than words can clarify. In a healthy family, people don't feel at home because certain phrases are used. People feel at home because they know others are glad to see them, show interest in them, and make it safe to talk about anything that is on their mind. Your demeanor will do as much to help your group transition from stage one to stage two as your words.

Feeling welcome is the leading factor in whether someone will return. For example, in an emotionally taxing group like *True Betrayal*, a group for those whose spouse has been unfaithful, a first-time guest might leave looking like they've had an exhausting "ugly cry." But if the welcomeness of the group allowed them to feel safe enough to be this vulnerable, there is a high likelihood that guest will return.

HOW ABOUT AFTER THE GROUP IS ESTABLISHED?

Once the core of your group is past stage one, you want to maintain the same welcoming response to new guests without detracting from the ability of established members to make progress. While these goals are in tension, they are not in contradiction.

The instructions on welcoming guests in chapter 5 covered the basics of balancing the needs of new guests and established members. Now we will consider how to navigate the relational dynamics in an open group when new participants arrive.

Participants who have begun the move from stage one to stage two, already have a sense of "us," a sense of who is committed to return each week and an awareness of each other's story. New participants disrupt this transition. Your goal as the group facilitator is to (a) name this disruption, (b) frame it positively, and (c) help mitigate its impact.

When participants sense there is something the leader is uncomfortable naming, mistrust emerges. Because of this emerging distrust, the change is viewed as "something wrong" instead of "something normal." That means that after your welcoming ritual, you might say something like this:

> "Welcoming new guests is a time when we see a good challenge in G4. It is easy to think that each of us being at a unique place on our journey is only good. It is good. It gives us a fresh perspective on where we've been (as we hear from those on earlier steps) and where we're going (as we hear from those on later steps).
>
> But we're not just on different points on our nine-step journey; we're also at different places in our trust of the group. Each time we welcome new participants, our new friends are starting to trust and our established members are expanding who they're willing to trust. If

> that's frustrating for you, don't feel ashamed or pressured. Learning healthy trust as we work on [group subject] is one of the most practical life lessons we learn in G4. Each time we welcome a new guest, we get to practice it afresh."

This kind of statement names and positively frames the impact of welcoming new guests. That, in and of itself, goes a long way toward mitigating the regression in trust that can come with welcoming new members.

There is a surprisingly simple strategy to help offset this potential trust regression: help established members bring new participants up to speed as they share. Part of the "us-ness" that emerges in group is the decreasing need to explain details in our story. When I can just say "Before my car accident," and know everyone remembers the story, I feel more at home. That is not just a matter of verbal efficiency, but also a matter of feeling known, a feeling that is essential to trust. New members disrupt this dynamic, but that is not their fault.

As a leader, you can mitigate this disruption by being watchful for moments when it is impacting the group. When a clarification is needed, you can help the established member still feel known by offering a brief summary of the background information relevant to what they shared. Doing so gives context to the new participant and prevents the established member from feeling like they must retell everything they have already said. Adding a word of commendation for the established member provides an additional buffer against potential disruption. For instance, you might say,

> "The car accident Kendal referenced was what prompted him to come to G4. I remember the first time you [Kendal] told us about that accident. It took a lot of courage then. Hearing you talk about it without the same emotional weight today shows how far you've come. I'm proud of you, and I'm grateful for you. Please continue with what you were sharing."

Once you have another member who begins to serve as coleader, you can ask them to look for these opportunities as well. That way you are not the only person serving as an encouraging historian for the group. The more you can affirm the courage and progress of group members, the more you create a culture where vulnerability and authenticity are normal. This demonstrates how navigating stage one well sets the group up to navigate its stage two and stage three hurdles.

WHAT IS THE GOAL OF STAGE ONE?

To summarize, the goal of stage one is to create a sense of "us," a sense of belonging. Until a participant knows who will be present each week and has embraced this as "their" group, progress toward their personal goals will be impeded. This requires you, as the G4 facilitator, to take the lead in helping the guest and established members grow comfortable with one another.

Chapter 19

STAGE TWO: NAVIGATING RESISTANCE TO CHANGE

It would be nice to think that after belonging (stage one) comes change. Unfortunately, that's frequently not true. Usually resistance comes after belonging. Why is that? Once we get over the distraction of not knowing the other people in group and figure out what to expect, we realize we must be honest with these people. The apprehension that accompanies vulnerability commonly expresses itself as resistance or conflict. This chapter is about equipping you to help your group navigate these obstacles.

WELCOME RESISTANCE

When we understand why resistance and conflict emerge, we realize they're a sign of growth. If participants were not considering being more honest, they wouldn't have the reflex to pull back. Feeling intimidated is the first part of courage. Where there is no internal angst, there is no need for courage. As leaders, we can learn to welcome resistance and conflict because they indicate something significant is on the brink of happening.

Think of it this way, *resistance is emotional honesty on the way to verbal honesty*. That is, we're feeling something we're not yet willing or able to put into words. Everyone knows that change is hard. That means we know we will question whether change is worth it in multiple ways at multiple points along our G4 journey. Having the courage to put this resistance into words is the next step toward progress.

As a G4 facilitator, we help individual participants and the group as a whole to navigate this challenge by welcoming it. *Welcoming resistance* requires recognizing resistance without taking it personally. What might resistance look like as your G4 group enters phase two? Signs of resistance appear in the following list:

- A participant may criticize the group curriculum or feedback from group members.
- A participant may show disinterest via surface level answers or sarcastic responses.
- A participant may develop a pattern of verbalizing exceptions to what anyone says.
- Conflict may emerge between members within the group.
- A participant may vilify their support network outside of group.
- A participant may attend but consistently not have done any homework.
- A participant may show an antagonistic or apathetic body posture that can negatively affect group dynamics.

As group leader, it is vital that you interpret these kinds of actions as being *to* you, not *at* you. That is what it means to *not personalize* resistance. Interpret these kinds of actions as saying, "I'm discouraged because change is hard and I'm not sure I want to continue," instead of, "This group is stupid, and the leader is doing a bad job."

In moments like these, your role as a G4 facilitator is like a sports coach managing the morale of a team when something goes wrong in a game. A player may make an error and think, *Great, I'm the worst player on the team.* Or a teammate might say, "You're the reason we're going to lose the game." Or the team as a whole might think, *There is no reason to continue to play hard because we don't have a chance.* In moments like these, the coach's job is to help the team weather the storm.

Your job as the group facilitator is to help your group persevere through moments of resistance and conflict. If the coach personalizes the rough patch saying, "Why won't you guys listen to me," or asking, "Do you guys not trust me as the coach?" the difficult moment gets worse. If the coach tries to overpower the situation with anger or ignores it, the situation gets worse. The same is true for your responses with the G4 group you lead.

So we welcome these challenges. The following paragraphs give examples of what welcoming resistance and conflict might sound like:

> "I get the sense that our motivation to change may be lower tonight than it has been in recent weeks. That happens. Some weeks we have more drive and hope than others. Does anyone else get that feeling from the group tonight? If so, can we talk about it?"

> "I get the sense you [particular group member] are frustrated. It's okay if you focus less on the curriculum tonight and more on what's bothering you. Honesty is always the first step toward anything getting better. What's going on?"

> "It seems like you [particular group member] are putting more energy toward finding exceptions than working on your journey. I get it. Change is hard and doesn't look the same for everyone. Is there something that prompted you to focus more on why you think things won't work?"

> [Conflict between group members] "It's awkward when we get snippy with each other. But it's inevitable when we're changing things that have been a large part of our lives. Plus, conflict like this frequently happens outside group. If we can resolve this conflict in group, it could help all of us resolve similar conflicts related to our struggle

> outside of group. Are we up for working on this conflict constructively?"

Each example does these three primary things:

1. Names the struggle in a noncombative way
2. Humanizes the person struggling or normalizes the struggle
3. Asks a question to foster a profitable conversation within the group

This is a general pattern you can follow when leading in difficult moments. Ignoring resistance detracts from the progress of everyone in group, not just the resistant person. But approaching resistance in these ways earns respect from the group (trusting you as the leader) and becomes an opportunity for participants to grow in their ability to navigate moments of resistance and conflict outside of group, a vital life skill for every member of the group.

Even if you can't yet name the dynamic, you can use this same outline to say something useful:

> "When something is hard or awkward in group, there are three things we need to do. First, we need to name what's going on. It's hard to resolve what we can't put into words. Second, we need to humanize the person struggling (they aren't our enemy) and normalize what is common in the struggle (2 Corinthians 10:13). Third, we need to find a question to serve as a productive entry point to a constructive conversation. Can we do that with this moment?"

In these kinds of conversations, your tone of voice and facial expression are key. You want to convey that you are not threatened by the awkward moment. G4 is a place where we must be comfortable talking about things that are not good. That's why we're here. When the group sees in your eyes and hears in your voice that you're not shaken, it creates the stability necessary to seek solutions.

GIVE PERIODIC PREEMPTIVE STATEMENTS

Resistance is common enough that we should speak to it often, even at times when resistance is not part of the group experience. Here are three times when you can preemptively help your group navigate stage two challenges.

First, after a particularly good evening of G4, you might commend the group and anticipate stage two challenges this way:

> "Tonight has been really good. I appreciate how honest and transparent each of you were. G4 is at its best on nights like tonight. There will be times when we're more reticent to share. When that happens, instead of feeling defeated or defensive, simply say, 'I'm not feeling as open to share as I have in the past.' We'll understand, appreciate your honesty, and pray for the courage to be as honest as we need to be."

Second, on an evening when you're reviewing one of the steps that is most vulnerable in your curriculum, you might say.

> "Tonight's material is weighty. I think it's going to stretch us in our vulnerability. Todd and Steve, you've each only been here a couple of weeks. Grow at your pace and don't feel rushed. But as we talk about this step, here's my challenge for tonight: *don't let half-truths stand as whole truths*. I'm not pressuring any of you to share more than you're comfortable, but if you leave out something that is pertinent to how you need to change, end with "There's more, but that's how much I'm comfortable sharing tonight." We understand. But it's important for each of us to acknowledge when we're sharing partial truths."

Third, when someone is graduating from group, invite them to reflect on when they most acutely felt the challenges of stage two.

> "Sherry, when someone graduates, it is exciting for all of us. We take hope from what God has done in your life. For those of us with more road on our G4 journey, do you mind sharing a couple of times that were pivotal to getting to where you are? Maybe there were times when you were wrestling with whether you were going to be honest enough with this group to allow God to do the work he wanted to do in your life here."

Statements like these normalize resistance in a healthy way, emphasize the importance of transparency, and provide verbal protocols for the group to navigate stage two challenges without it feeling like a confrontation. Making these kinds of statements along the way allows the vignettes that directly addressed moments of resistance to seem less abnormal.

MAINTAIN TEAM MORALE

Returning to the coaching metaphor, in stage two your role is to help the group maintain focus and morale as they adapt to the heightened honesty of a G4 group. In that sense, your best tool is a compassionate smile as you move toward the awkward moment.

A good coach doesn't know everything that is going to happen in a game. No one could. Similarly, you can't predict the moments of resistance that may emerge in group. But a good coach maintains the trust of the team by being honest about the situation, identifying needed adjustments, and calling each player to remain focused on the goal. That is your role when stage two challenges emerge in group.

Chapter 20

STAGE THREE: CREATING A SHARED CULTURE

A foundation of honesty and vulnerability (stage two) allows you to build a culture (stage three) suited to facilitate change (stage four). We need to remember that each stage is not an island disconnected from the others, but part of a continuous process.

As we trace our journey to stage three, we see that stage one is exciting—people are showing up and the opportunity to start a group is emerging. Stage two is hard but worth it as you manage the tension that comes with increased honesty. Stage three is encouraging again as you get a sense that cohesion is emerging in the group.

TRANSITIONING FROM "US" TO "OURS"

In stage one, participants were gaining a sense of belonging to the group. Now in stage three they are building a sense of *mutual ownership* of the group. We can call this the transition from "us" to "ours." In stage three, members begin to think beyond themselves and grow in their concern for the progress of others in the group. Group members begin to trust one another and seek each other's counsel about their struggle (Romans 15:14). Members share openly within the group and are willing to hear and accept feedback from other members (James 5:16).

In stage three, your role as the leader becomes less central to the life of the group, but no less important. You may begin to feel that this group could run without you. That is like the moment when a parent is proud of their teenager's growing independence. It is, and should be, satisfying, but it doesn't mean your role is complete.

SURRENDERING CONTROL FOR CO-OWNERSHIP

This transition may feel awkward for you. In stage one, you were an active leader. In stage two, you helped the group articulate their own resistance and navigate the resulting conflict(s). These roles feel more like leading. From stage three forward, you will transition from *leading* to *facilitating*. The longer you can stay in the facilitating role, the healthier the group is. At G4, facilitating is the ideal role for the leader.

This transition from leader to facilitator is the difference between being a *good leader* at G4 and a *great leader*. Faithful volunteers are wonderful and needed. A ministry can persist when only the leader feels ownership of the group. But if you cling to too much control in stage three, you won't multiply yourself and you'll stifle the growth of your group. Ironically, great G4 leaders are willing to transition from being leaders to being facilitators.

By way of metaphor, the transition from leader to facilitator is like the difference between playing lead guitar in a band and conducting an orchestra. When you play lead guitar, you're the star and everyone else in the band adapts to you. When you're the conductor, your role is to maintain rhythm and harmony. As you enter stage three, that is a good picture of your emerging role. We want you to be excited, not threatened, as you see this happening. No one is replacing you. You are seeing the group itself mature—not just members within the group. That is a good thing.

On any given night at G4, you will still guide the evening, prompting when one part of the group experience gives way to the next. But during times of sharing and offering feedback, you will be more encourager than teacher. You will be highlighting what is good in the disclosures and feedback from group members more than doing the primary commenting.

That means in stage three you begin to wait longer to comment after someone shares to allow other group members to encourage or offer perspective. When they do, the focus of your words is affirming and developing the members offering feedback. Members are cultivating growth in one another, and you are encouraging and developing members' ability to care for one another in group. Your comments might sound like these:

> "Becky, I really like what you said to Susan. Noticing how she articulated her fears without embracing her fears is so important. When we can see this in each other, it means we are really understanding the process. Susan, thank you for sharing so openly, and Becky, thank you for how you encouraged her."

> "Jerry, I'm so glad you remembered what it used to be like for Neale to talk about his anger. Neale, you have grown a lot. One of the great things about G4 is that the longer we are in group, the more we can catch each other doing things better. Having people who remember the beginning of our journey can help us remain encouraged about where we are now."

> "Grace reminded me before group tonight that today is the three-year anniversary of Christy losing her daughter. I asked Christy if it would be okay if we spent some time praying for her and telling some of the things we admire about her journey with us. She said she would like that. Grace, thank you for thinking of Christy this way."

The principle here is to *let no good comment go unaffirmed*. Anything counseling related tends to be negative. After all, we come to counseling to grow in areas of life that are bad (sinful) or hard (suffering). We counter this propensity to be negative by looking for moments of growth.

Early in the life of the group during stages one and two, you, as the leader, will likely have to set the example of affirming growth. Then, as you enter stage three, other members will have embraced this aspect of G4 culture, and your encouragement can focus on affirming the care between members.

NEW MEMBERS AND REGRESSION AFTER STAGE THREE

Like any other stage of development in an open group, you can see a regression in stage three as new participants arrive. That is both good and sad (not bad). As you imagine your group reaching stage three, it should make you sad to think of there being a regression. But progress through these stages in an open group is like the incoming ocean tide; there is a lot of forward and backward, but also a clear sense of direction.

The reality is that new participants are not ready to interact at a stage three level. They do not know others and are not known well enough by the others in the group. This is not bad, but it is an obstacle to be navigated so that it does not disrupt the maturation of the group or the progress of participants. To use another metaphor, stage three interactions are like playing jazz. Strangers can't play jazz together. That is not because they are not individually good musicians, but because jazz entails knowing the melody of the song and making adaptations to how that melody is played as each instrumentalist adjusts to the others. It takes time to develop that kind of relationship. New participants need some time to experience the group before they can join in at the level the group has reached.

In an open group, the quality of feedback that each person gets will not be equal. That is, members who have been in the group longer will get feedback tailored to their experience more often than participants who are new to the group. Newer participants will get feedback that is more generic or directed to their struggle instead of their overall story. That isn't a function of established members being more popular, but new participants being less known.

If established members try to offer the same quality of feedback to newer participants, it will result in more guessing and filling in details of the participant's story with assumptions. That creates the awkwardness that comes with feeling misunderstood or stereotyped.

As the G4 facilitator, this means you will interact with each member based on where they are in their developing relationship with the group. This is clearest with first-time guests. You care for them in stage one ways. No one thinks that is awkward because everyone knows it's necessary. But when you have stage two members in a group where the majority of members are at stage three or four, it can be awkward. It becomes less clear that caring for these members in stage two ways is good.

When you have stage two participants in a mature group, you should respond sooner to their sharing. By contrast, you wait longer to respond to members at a stage three or four relationship with the group. This prevents guessing by the rest of the group and allows them to respond to each other in ways that are most instinctual to where their relationship is with the group.

As you mentor a coleader or have long-term members in the group, explain to them why and how you are being intentional. Their ability to join you in this intentional style of interaction is a good indicator they are ready to take on more leadership in the group.

USING YOUR PRIMARY TOOLS: MODELING, AFFIRMATION, AND PAUSES

As a G4 leader, you have three primary tools to help you navigate the challenge of facilitating a group where participants are at various stages: modeling, affirmation, and pauses.

You help your *initial members* mature to a stage three level of engagement through **modeling**. The best way to invite people to be honest and transparent is to be honest and transparent with them.

Conversely, the best way to teach people to be fake and closed is to be fake and closed with them.

Think of honest, nondefensive disclosures about our life struggles as the second language people are learning at G4, much like English speakers learning Spanish or French. Your sharing at a stage three level of vulnerability is the best way to help the group become proficient in this new language.

You encourage *established members* to provide stage three level feedback through **affirmation**. As you offer stage three feedback, other members will do the same. When they do, affirm their feedback to their peers. The general ministry principle, we replicate what we celebrate, holds true here. When you hear one group member respond to another group member in an uplifting and edifying way (your previous role in stages one and two), use your words to affirm the member who stepped into your role to acknowledge that this is the desired normal for the group.

You help *newer members* catch up to the rest of the group by the intentional use of **pauses** after various members share. Don't be afraid of silence. An experienced group leader will realize that their pauses can be as intentional and effective as their words in orchestrating the group's growth.

When experienced members share, intentionally wait to be the second or third speaker so that you can affirm those who respond well. When less tenured members share, offer feedback based on their attachment to the group. Taking this approach helps members relating to the group at a stage three level mature, while preventing members at a stage two level from feeling rushed.

The first three stages lay the foundation for change. Cultivating belonging, navigating resistance, and establishing a shared culture create a fertile environment for change to happen. That's where we'll turn our attention next.

Chapter 21

STAGE FOUR: DOING THE HARD WORK OF CHANGE

In G4, stage four is the goal of previous work. We want to see lives transformed through the biblical teaching and gospel application of each curriculum. We want to see people find freedom from the entanglement of sin and comfort from the impact of suffering. Stages one, two, and three have brought us to the point of seeing these dreams realized.

FALLING FROM HEAVEN

There is the classic scene in the movie *Field of Dreams*[1] where a ghostly baseball player comes through a cornfield, walks onto a pristine baseball field awkwardly nestled in the middle of Iowa, and asks, "Is this heaven?" Because the field seemed too good to be true he assumed it was heaven. If we're not careful, we can talk about stage four of a G4 group in comparably idealistic language. Stage four isn't heaven, but it may be as close as we get in G4.

When established members of a group reach a stage four, they will share a strong bond with one another, be committed to the process of change, be honest about their struggles, and encourage each other in their journeys. Hearing their weekly updates will be

1. Robinson, Phil Alden. *Field of Dreams*. Universal Pictures, 1989.

an encouragement to you. Seeing them care for one another will inspire you. The group will truly feel like family.

The positive energy of stage four helps us understand why setbacks and relapses are so intensely discouraging at this point. Setbacks hurt worse after a member has experienced stage four for these two reasons:

First, the participant is disappointing themselves; they have now known freedom. Before G4, their struggle seemed inevitable. Now they know freedom is possible. That makes a setback sting worse.

Second, the participant may also feel like they failed the group. Once G4 feels like family and we've celebrated many growth markers together, we don't want to say, "I did *it* again." When we didn't care about the people in group and we didn't think they cared about us, that statement didn't hurt as badly. Now it feels like telling your children you cheated on their mom or dad.

As a G4 leader, when the group has reached stage four and an established member has a setback, it is another time when you speak early. Don't rush, talk fast, or talk loudly. But do speak first because your voice has an important role to play in reestablishing the equilibrium of the group. You might say something like this:

> "Jonathan, we hurt *for* you, and we hurt *with* you. You've been enough like a brother to us all that it may be hard for some of us not to personalize your setback. Tonight is going to feel different for us all. But the main thing we ask of each other at G4 is to be honest. You've done that, and we thank you. If you're willing and as much as you're able, would you share with us where you are now and how we can support you? [Listen.] I think many of us are stunned because, while we've all said this could easily be us, we realize it in a fresh way now. From that perspective, does anyone want to encourage Jonathan? [Listen.] We would be foolish not to do a rugged self-assessment on a night

like tonight. Are there any half-truths or compromises that others of us realize we need to disclose?" [Listen.]

In this vignette, you are working to prevent the surprise of this established member's setback from changing the culture of the group. Undoubtedly, it will change the atmosphere of the evening. But as with other challenges, you name what's going on, humanize the experience (both for the group member who experienced the setback and for the other group members), and provide questions to help the group begin productively exploring the experience.

If a person lets you know of a setback in advance, as may often be the case, you can alter the natural rhythms of the group and prepare the other participants to hear what their friend has to say. It might sound like this:

> "Tonight we're going to start a little differently. Jonathan reached out to me yesterday and shared something he wants to share with the group. This will feel like a heavy way for us to start, but I appreciate Jonathan's integrity and courage in calling me. Jonathan . . . "

The emotional high of stage four provides both an incredible view of God's grace and a painful place to fall from. Your role as the G4 facilitator is to help the group harvest as much progress from the stage four time as possible when it's good and prevent as much regression as possible when stage four is disrupted. We'll look at two more ways to cultivate progress and then one more disruption you are likely to navigate.

TASKS: TAILORED AFFIRMATION AND DIFFERENTIATION

When established members are relating to the group at a stage four level, there is much opportunity for **affirmation**. You might feel more like a cheerleader (i.e., encourager) than a group leader. That is great, but we don't want to waste the enthusiasm by being generic.

Think in terms of Isaac Newton's first law of motion—an object in motion tends to stay in motion. Group members are moving in stage four. You want to be intentional with your responses to build momentum and refine the direction for that motion. You might say things like the following:

> "Claire, what encourages me in what you just said is that you're starting to be as honest with people outside of group as you are here at G4. The way you trusted your sister was beautiful. That means G4 isn't just a ministry you attend, but a lifestyle that you are starting to embrace. It is exciting and challenging to see you grow that way."

> "Mark, I appreciate your willingness to return to step 3. Sometimes we get so focused on reaching step 9 that we resist revisiting earlier steps. But when you realized that there was a new motive vying to draw you back into addiction, you didn't ignore it. You refused to view revisiting step 3 as a setback. Thank you for that courage and example."

> "Amy, I know we're here to talk about depression, but hearing you apply what you've learned about depression to your experience of grief was really insightful. You reminded me that we're not just here to "not be depressed" but to respond to all our unpleasant emotions in a way that honors God. Thank you for showing that we can honor God with our down emotions."

Each of these affirmations is tailored to highlight aspects of growth that would be easy for Claire, Mark, Amy, and other members of the group to miss. From a G4 perspective, these areas of growth are extracurricular, meaning they would not be found in the curriculum. But as the group facilitator, during stage four you are looking for evidence of growth to affirm.

Your other stage four tool is **differentiation**. The premise here is that while we are all on the same journey, we do not all take the same path. We share a common beginning to our journey, which is the topic for the group. We share a common end to our journey, which is greater freedom from our struggle. But much can be different in between. As the group leader, you can help group members avoid the mentality of hearing each other's testimonies as prescriptions. You can say things like the following:

> "Jordan, I can't help but notice how different your step 1 work was from Candace's. Your preparation for the journey focused on regulating your schedule so that your sleeping and eating habits were normal. Candace, remember how you worked so hard on inviting a couple of friends to know your struggle so you felt less alone? It's worth remembering that while we're working through the same steps, our journeys will be different."

> "Frank, it's interesting that while you and Bob have expressed your anger in similar ways and at the same kinds of people in your lives, your step 3 motives are quite different. For you, anger is a way to try to regain control, while Bob used it as an attempt to punish people when he didn't get the respect he thought he deserved. It's important to see how we can be challenged by each other's honesty without trying to mimic each other's journey."

These kinds of statements help the group understand what they should be gleaning from each other sharing at G4. A naive view of G4 would think that because we are using the same nine steps and the same curriculum, we learn from those ahead of us *what* we should do next. Sometimes that happens, if our personalities and situations are similar. More often, we are challenged by each other's honesty and that compels us to engage the curriculum more authentically. Periodically making comments like the ones above helps group members remember this.

MANAGING THE DISCOURAGEMENT OF NEW MEMBERS

The closeness among members who have developed a stage four relationship with the group can create a sense of discouragement for people newer to the group. Seeing the trust, hearing their vulnerability, and noting their rate of progress can have an "I'll never get there" effect. Stage four can be so good that it's intimidating to those who are at earlier stages in their relationship with the group.

Like other dynamics we've discussed, this isn't bad. It's another challenge to be navigated. In this case, you can use affirmation accompanied by a question to invite experienced members to reflect on their journey as a way to encourage newer participants. It might sound like this.

> "Philip, I think it can be easy to miss how much growth is represented, not only in what you shared, but in how comfortably you shared it. You showed a remarkable trust for the group when talking about your weaknesses. For those of us who haven't been a part of this group as long, do you mind sharing with us how you grew to this level of comfort?"

Note the "us" language in the second half of the vignette. As the leader, you will have been part of the group longer than Philip, but you are speaking for the benefit of those who have only recently started attending G4, so you speak in a way that identifies with them.

Further, inviting established members to articulate how they grew over time to trust the group helps newer members feel less rushed. It would be easy for these newer members to wonder, *Can I be* that *honest?* Putting this apprehension into words affirms for these newer members that it is okay for each participant to be at *both* a different place in the nine steps *and* a different place in their relationship with the group.

STEWARDING THE GOOD OF STAGE FOUR

When members of your group reach stage four, there will be so much to celebrate. It is an exciting time of substantive growth in the lives of people you've been praying for during the last weeks or months. It is right and appropriate to cherish the encouragement that comes from the fruit of your labor.

However, this chapter has focused more on the challenges that can emerge during this time because it is easy to become so distracted by the good that is happening that you lose your posture of continuing to guide the group through the ups and downs of adding new members and facing the inevitable setbacks of existing members.

If you can take a both-and mentality—celebrate growth and keep an eye on challenges—into stage four, you have gotten what you need from this chapter. To adapt Romans 12:15 to this stage of group maturation, this is a time when you, "Rejoice with those who are rejoicing over what God is doing in their life, weep with those who feel shame over a setback, and comfort those who are intimidated by those who have been in the group longer."

Chapter 22

STAGE FIVE: GRADUATING AND CELEBRATING FRIENDS

G4 groups aren't designed to last forever—at least, they're not designed for participants to stay in as their ongoing source of discipleship. When members reach their goals and demonstrate they can solidify their progress, they should graduate into the general discipleship ministries of your church.

Having someone graduate from G4 is both exciting and a bit sad. It is exciting to celebrate a major achievement. This person came to G4 because of a life-dominating struggle with sin or suffering. They are graduating having seen significant, sustained progress with that struggle. That's a big deal!

It is a bit sad because we won't see them weekly at G4 anymore. We will miss them. It is not that we will never see them again. It is likely that we will see them around church, and if we've developed a friendship, it is perfectly appropriate to hang out as friends.[1] We just won't see them at G4 each week, and this will leave a void for a while.

---

1. To be as intentional in these friendships as you've been in G4, consider my book *Transformative Friendships: 7 Questions to Deepen Any Relationship* (Greensboro, NC: New Growth Press, 2024).

GRADUATION VS. "AS NEEDED"

If we wanted to be precise, we would say that our friend who is concluding their G4 journey is going to an "as-needed basis" with the group, meaning they are welcome to come back whenever they like. However, transitioning to an "as-needed basis" doesn't generate the same celebratory tone as "graduation," so we recommend you have a graduation ceremony!

There are several reasons a G4 graduate might visit or return to the group.

- To support or celebrate with a friend in group who is reaching a milestone.
- At the request of the G4 leader, to share their testimony for the benefit of the group.
- To help navigate a difficult season when a "G4 booster" would serve them well.
- If they experience a setback and need to resume being a consistent member.

It is wise to clarify with the group that while we use the term *graduation*, this isn't like high school where once you graduate, you aren't allowed to return. If graduation feels too final, it may create apprehension that distracts from the growth opportunities and celebration we want to cultivate with each graduation.

DO RECOVERY GROUPS GRADUATE MEMBERS?

If you've been around recovery ministries, you may be asking *should people really graduate from groups like G4?* Historically, groups like G4—especially those focused on addiction—have used the mantra "once an addict, always an addict" and have advised people against discontinuing participation in the group. If you have group members with a recovery background, they may feel like graduation is a disservice to their fellow group members.

In the context of groups like Alcoholics Anonymous (AA), this advice makes sense and is wise. In AA, there are two options for participants: (a) continue to be in group, or (b) be isolated without support or accountability. If those are the only options, it is wiser to never graduate. However, those are not the only two options in G4.

G4 is intentionally embedded in local churches. During steps 8 and 9, participants are instructed to evaluate and cultivate meaningful relationships of mutual support with church members outside of G4. Until these relationships are established, someone is not ready to graduate. But once these relationships are established, a G4 graduate is not moving from a context of support to isolation. They are moving from targeted accountability and support (the subject of the group) to broad accountability and support. Intentionality during the pre-graduation phase ensures that these relationships are not superficial.

Having G4 graduates take the honesty and authenticity of G4 into the general discipleship ministries of your church is a way that G4 blesses the church. As more and more people graduate from G4 into the general discipleship ministries of a church, it begins to "raise the temperature" on discipleship in your church.

SCRIPT FOR A GRADUATION MEETING

A graduation night should be announced in advance, and most of the people who will speak during the evening should be given directions on their role. Once you've had several people graduate, the flow and flavor of the evening should become an established part of the culture.

While you should adapt this outline to fit each graduate and the culture of your group, here is a basic template you can work from when planning a G4 graduation night:

- Tell the story of G4.
- Invite the graduate to tell about their G4 journey.
- Invite group members to affirm and encourage the graduate.
- Pray for and commission the graduate.
- Take time for fellowship and casual celebration.

We'll detail each part. Think of yourself as the emcee for the evening.

Part One: Telling the G4 Story

Graduations are a time to recast the vision for G4. Most of our vision-casting is done from a beginning or middle of the journey perspective. We cast vision to rally motivation for moments that are hard. Graduations provide an opportunity to cast vision from an end of the journey perspective as we celebrate the fruit of this ministry.

During this part of the evening, which should last three to five minutes, you might say something like this:

> "Tonight is a special night at G4. Most nights we meet to encourage each other on our journey. Tonight we're here to celebrate that Omar is completing his G4 journey. Omar has been where each of you is, and, by God's grace, he is currently where each of us is striving to be. It is not that his sanctification journey is complete. God still has much to do in and through Omar. But the goals he set for his time at G4 have been reached, and we want to celebrate that.
>
> We each came to G4 because we knew there was something we couldn't overcome without God's help and the support of fellow believers. It is amazing to think that, as hard as it was for us to admit we needed to be here, it becomes equally hard for us to see Omar leave. We don't just grow as individuals here; we grow together, and the bond of this group is a big part of what God uses to foster our growth.
>
> Tonight is a time when we look back and we look forward. *We look back* and celebrate what God has done in Omar's life. We look back and reflect on what Omar has meant to each of us personally. We look back and remember where we started our G4 journey and gain fresh encouragement about how far we've come. *We look forward* in anticipation of what's next for Omar and what God wants to do in our own lives.

To get us started on this looking back and looking forward, I've asked Omar to share his full G4 journey and give us any charge that God has laid on his heart. We've all heard pieces of Omar's story as he's shared in group, but tonight we're going to get to hear the "puzzle box top," rather than just look at a few pieces."

Part Two: The Graduate Telling about Their G4 Journey

For the group, this is the highlight of the evening. So much of the G4 experience is staccato as we hear brief snippets of people's story and struggle. As people share at G4, it is as if we are watching short scenes from different movies with different characters in quick succession. On this night, we get to watch one movie from start to finish as our friend tells their story.

This part of the evening might last between ten and fifteen minutes. Many participants may not have thought through the entirety of their stories from beginning to end. During hardships, most of us focus only on the things immediately in front of us. The questions below serve as prompts for your graduate to think through as they prepare what they will share.

- What brought you to G4?
- How did you try to convince yourself that you didn't need to come?
- What was the point where you committed to the group?
- What was the biggest challenge or discouragement after that point?
- What were the changes you made that had the biggest impact?
- When did this group begin to feel like family?
- As you made progress, what things became harder than you expected?
- What adjustments did you need to make to offset these new challenges?
- Which key moments did God show up in ways that exceeded your expectations?

- What moments were drier than you expected?
- What will you miss most about G4?
- What are you most excited about investing your time and energy in as you graduate G4?
- How can we pray for you?

Not every graduate will directly answer each question. But this list tries to capture the rise and fall of an authentic growth process, while capturing both the stages of personal growth (i.e., the nine steps) and stages of group development.

Part Three: Members Affirming and Encouraging the Graduate

After the graduate shares their journey, transition to a time of encouragement when members affirm what they have learned from and admired about this person during their time in G4.

Each person should strive to limit their remarks to two to three minutes. Let the group know the week before that the following week will be a graduation meeting, so they can think through what they want to say. Based on the size of the group, this part of the graduation may take fifteen to twenty minutes. If the group is smaller, then each member could be encouraged to share more. Here are a series of prompts for this time:

- The part of your story that challenged/encouraged me most is…
- [Blank] is something you said that I will always remember and has been very helpful to me.
- You may not remember the night when [event] happened, but you said/did [blank] and it [describe personal impact].
- During my time at G4 I've grown to appreciate [character quality] about you.
- I don't want you to graduate without hearing me affirm/appreciate [blank] about you.

The goal of this time is to help the graduate realize that not only was their life changed at G4, but that their participation in G4 also changed other people's lives. As the remaining group members hear this time of sharing, there will be a growing appreciation for what this group means to each of them.

Part Four: Praying for and Commissioning the Graduate

When the graduate tells their story, it should conclude with what they are excited about for their future. Whatever is next should be a significant focus during prayer time.

You might have the graduate sit in a chair in the middle of the group and invite the other members to lay hands on them to commission the graduate for the goals and dreams God has for them. The most important thing is not the arrangement of the room, but for the graduate to know they are being sent out by the group and that the group is excited for them.

Part Five: Taking Time for Fellowship and Casual Celebration

There are some things that are done best in the rhythms of a ceremony. There are other things that are done best in the non-rhythms of casual celebration. For this reason, it is good to have food and time to just hang out on a graduation night. This atmosphere allows for a different type of sharing, relaxing, laughing, affirming, crying, storytelling, reflecting, and other interactions that foster a sense that this graduate's journey is complete.

As the group leader, take time to relish these moments. You were an instrument of God's grace in this person's life. Savor the fruit of your labor. There will be enough discouragement over participants who don't reach this point, that savoring these moments is an important part of nourishing your soul.

Chapter 23

JOB DESCRIPTION OF A G4 FACILITATOR

As you read this job description, there shouldn't be any surprises. It is an opportunity to review everything we've talked about in the previous twenty-two chapters and see your key responsibilities succinctly summarized in a few pages. The more you read this job description and think, *Yeah, that's what I understand my role to be*, the more ready you are to begin the adventure of being a G4 facilitator.

G4 facilitators do many things, but their role can be summed up in one sentence: *Be present weekly, guiding the group as each member walks their individual journey of change through the group's curriculum.*

If you plan to take on this role, we ask you to prepare by doing the following three things:

- Read the manual for G4 group leaders, *Facilitating Church-Based Counseling Groups* (i.e., this book). Good news—you've almost completed this step!
- Study and familiarize yourself with your group's curriculum. You don't have to be an expert on the subject (addiction, depression, trauma, etc.). But you do need to be familiar enough with the curriculum to facilitate the group and answer basic participant questions.

- Participate in a small group within the church's discipleship ministry that cares for you as a local missionary. It is recommended that you participate not as a leader but as a regular member of the group. This is for your emotional and relational stamina. We hope you will lead your G4 group long enough to see dozens of people complete their full journey. Self-care is an important part of that kind of perseverance (more on this in appendix C).

Once you become a group leader, you will need to:

- Be present for the majority of G4 nights each year to lead your group. Your consistent presence is essential to having a healthy group culture and high participant retention. Set the standard for being on time, prepared, and enthusiastic.
- Communicate with your G4 director[1] when needs emerge that are more severe than your group is prepared to address. If someone needs more help than your group can offer, your G4 director will help you identify where additional help can be found in your community.
- If your church has a collection of G4 groups, serve as needed in the welcome and large group times. These roles require minimal preparation, but when done well, they contribute significantly to a healthy G4 culture. Your G4 director will coordinate these needs.
- Greet and orient new participants for your group (see chapters 7, 12, and 18).
- Model authenticity and honesty during group discussions (see chapters 19–20).
- Monitor the growth of individuals in the group (see chapters 13–15) and the development of the group as a whole (see section three). The next section of this job description offers several questions that can help you gauge how your group is doing.

---

1. If your church only has one or two groups and, therefore, does not have a G4 director, a designated member of the pastoral staff should fill this role.

- Identify maturing member(s) of your group who can serve as coleader. Vet this possibility with your G4 director. When you both agree that an individual is a good candidate to be a coleader, ask them to begin reading *Facilitating Church-Based Counseling Groups*.
- Once you identify a coleader, you should begin to read *Mobilizing Church-Based Counseling* as part of your continuing education as a G4 leader. This will further develop you as a leader and equip you to answer more of your new coleader's questions.

The content above is arranged as a typical, bullet-point-driven job description. It is a list of tasks and trainings. But we can also conceptualize a job description by providing you with questions to gauge the health of your group. Let's examine five questions that will help you think through the group's health. These questions should be frequent topics of conversation between you and your G4 director and coleader.

1. HOW MANY PEOPLE ARE IN YOUR G4 GROUP?

Ideally, groups would have between six and twelve participants in addition to you and a coleader. When a group nears fifteen participants, you need to multiply into two groups, with your previous coleader leading the emerging group and each of you beginning to look for new coleaders.

When a group is smaller than five participants, it can be more difficult to maintain morale and function like a group. Until your group consistently reaches this critical mass, conversations with your G4 director should focus on how to raise awareness for the group within your church and community.

2. WHERE IS THE GROUP IN ITS COLLECTIVE DEVELOPMENTAL CYCLE?

As we've noted, most G4 groups are open groups. That means you may answer this question in several different ways. You might say, "The six members who have been here the longest are consistently at stage four, and actually two of them are close to graduating. We have a couple of newer participants who are moving between stages two and three. And the newest guest is still at stage one. That means much of our group discussion has a stage four flavor with occasional stage two conflicts emerging."

Discussing this question periodically with your coleader and G4 director is an excellent way to maintain awareness of your group's development. Because no one gives weekly updates on how the group is doing (like each individual member does about their progress), it is easy to miss the maturation of the group as a whole.

3. WHERE IS EACH GROUP MEMBER?

Monitoring the group as a whole doesn't mean neglecting the individual members of the group. When your G4 director asks you, "Where are the members in your group on their journey?" You should be able to answer something like this:

> "We currently have seven members who are committed to the group and making progress through the curriculum. Two members are currently working on step 8. I'm keeping an eye on when they may be ready to graduate. Two others are on step 6. Then there is one member each on steps 3, 4, and 5. We've had a couple of new guests lately, but they haven't made it past step 1 yet, so I don't know if they'll stick."

As the group leader, you should be able to put names with each of those people. But when you're talking to someone outside the group, anonymous updating is more appropriate.

For groups that are using non-nine-step curriculums, you would not be able to update with clear step designations as in the example above. In these cases, you might say something like this:

> "We have eight people committed to the group. Five of them have been here for several months. They own their struggle, are not defensive talking about challenges, and

they are committed to engaging the curriculum for guidance on how to grow. The other three still get discouraged quickly when change is hard, and then they can be defensive about it. I'm worried about whether one has the level of commitment to stick in the group, but the other two work through their defensiveness well and get reoriented toward their goals. I think that once they get further in the curriculum, they will be where the majority of the group is."

This doesn't use nine-step language, but it still shows awareness of where participants are in their personal journeys.

4. WHAT GOOD THINGS IN YOUR GROUP CAN WE CELEBRATE?

Leading a G4 group can be an emotionally weighty experience. While rewarding, you will hear a disproportionate number of life hardships. As the leader, you may find this draining. One of the best things you can do for your fellow G4 leaders and that your G4 director can do for you is ask, "What good things worth celebrating have happened in your group recently?" This question keeps us from fixating on the challenges that emerge in group to the point that we neglect seeing the good God is doing through the group. You might answer with something like the following:

"I found someone I think will make a great coleader."

"The level of trust between members has increased significantly in the last couple of weeks."

"Last weekend, a member who previously relapsed a couple of times reached out to people in the group instead of succumbing to temptation."

"We have a participant who has never been part of a church before. As she is entering step 4, she is beginning to realize that the Bible isn't a spiritual self-help book, but rather an invitation to a relationship with Jesus. Everyone in the group is excited to see her begin to get it."

Giving these reports is as good for your soul as it is informative for the other person. As G4 leaders, we need to be reminded to have eyes to see the *good* that is happening amid the *hard* and *bad* that we're navigating. This is a unique benefit that emerges when you have multiple G4 groups meeting on the same night at the same location. It allows for more of this kind of peer support and encouragement between leaders.

5. WHAT HARD THINGS IN YOUR GROUP CAN I HELP YOU NAVIGATE?

Question four doesn't mean you have to wear rose-colored glasses. Good things don't negate hard things. Both can—and usually do—coexist in the same group at the same time. Being a healthy leader of a healthy group requires being honest about both.

Hard things your group could encounter may look like the following situations:

> "We've had a couple of people drop out of group recently. Both got discouraged by setbacks and then quit coming. That's made our attendance fall below the threshold of feeling like a 'group' when we've had a couple of weeks with only three people present. It's been hard for the group and hard for me."

> "We're in that phase where several people are learning to trust the group, but don't trust the group yet. That means we've got more awkward moments than usual, and it's not fun."

> "I need a coleader and one hasn't emerged yet. I'm getting tired and I'm feeling the pressure of not being able to ever miss a week."

Conversations like these may result in the other person offering a creative idea that leads to relief, or it may simply allow a leader to feel heard and supported during a hard season. Either way, your longevity as a leader (and the longevity of other leaders) will be enhanced when this question is asked often. Additionally, the quality of your group will improve as you collectively brainstorm responses to things that are hard.

CONCLUSION

Being a group leader doesn't mean being a superhero. You're human too. The questions above aren't a report card. Considering these questions will help both you and your group to grow. And discussing these questions with your coleader and director invites mutual support and problem-solving for the things that are hard in your ministry.

Appendix A

G4 SERIES NINE-STEP CURRICULUMS

While a G4 ministry can and is highly encouraged to utilize group-based counseling curriculums from other authors,[1] this appendix lists the G4 nine-step curriculum options and links to the video-based presentations of this content. Having several groups utilizing these curriculums helps participants understand why the elements of your opening G4 "big group time" are structured as they are. (The layout of an evening of G4 is discussed in *Facilitating Counseling Groups*.)

Note: After the publication of *Mobilizing,* each G4 curriculum will be published progressively by New Growth Press. Until a published edition of each curriculum is available, a printable PDF version will be available and can be requested at the links below.

False Love

For chronic struggle with pornography, sexual addiction, and adultery

www.bradhambrick.com/falselove

1. A list of possible curriculums is at available at "Possible Curriculum for a G4 Ministry," bradhambrick.com/G4curriculum. In addition, chapter 15 of *Facilitating* contains further guidance on vetting and selecting curriculums that do not use the G4 nine-step models.

True Betrayal

For the spouse of someone engaged in a chronic struggle with pornography, sexual addiction, and adultery

www.bradhambrick.com/truebetrayal

Overcoming Addiction

For substance-related addiction, although it could be used as a separate group for behavior addictions like gambling

www.bradhambrick.com/addiction

Navigating Destructive Relationships

For someone navigating the aftermath of a relationship marked by addiction or abuse

www.bradhambrick.com/destructive

Post-Traumatic Stress

www.bradhambrick.com/ptsd

Disordered Eating

For individuals struggling with overeating or restricting, but should be different groups

www.bradhambrick.com/healthy

Overcoming Depression–Anxiety[2]

www.bradhambrick.com/depression

Overcoming Anger

www.bradhambrick.com/anger

2. The emotions of depression and anxiety are addressed as one topic because the co-occurrence rate of these emotions is so high. For severe struggles with either emotion (for example, suicidal ideation or acute phobias), G4 alone would not be an adequate form of care. This group would, at most, be supplemental care for individuals with severe struggles with only one of these emotions.

Appendix B

WHAT TO DO WHEN SOMETHING GOES BAD-BAD

These are the moments that make churches skittish about starting a counseling ministry. That is understandable. Counseling ministries engage with the most broken parts of our life, and it is easiest for things to go from bad to crisis in already broken situations. However, this four-step crisis response plan should feel both intuitive and doable in light of what you've been learning in *Facilitating* and, especially with your G4 director and church leadership already having worked through *Mobilizing*.

STEP ONE: KNOW YOUR IMMEDIATE REPORT SCENARIOS

In two scenarios you need to be prepared to involve outside authorities: (a) reasonable suspicion of child abuse or neglect and (b) threats of immediate harm to self or another person. To prepare for these two possibilities, your G4 director and pastor overseeing this ministry should have a joint phone call or in-person meeting with both Child Protective Services (CPS) and your local law enforcement office. Recommendations for each conversation follow below.

1. CPS for the reasonable suspicion of child abuse or neglect.[1]
    - » Introduce yourself and let them know you are calling to get information, not report an instance of abuse. This may affect where your call is directed.
    - » Thank them for their service in your community.
    - » Briefly describe the G4 ministry you are starting as the reason for your call.
    - » Ask them to describe situations when and how a report would need to be made.
    - » Ask them to explain what happens when a report of abuse is made.
    - » Ask them what happens after a report is made.
    - » Ask how they would want you to support a victim of abuse or neglect.
    - » Ask how they would want you to respond if the abuser was in your group.
    - » Ask if they have someone who would be willing to do a Q&A at a pastoral staff meeting or G4 leader debrief.
    - » Ask them what other questions they wish pastors and religious communities would ask them.
    - » Thank them again for their service to your community.

2. Local law enforcement office to discuss response to a threat of harm to self or others.

    - » Introduce yourself and let them know you are calling to get information, not report a crime. This may affect where your call is directed.
    - » Thank them for their service in your community.
    - » Briefly describe the G4 ministry you are starting as the reason for your call.

---

1. It is recommended that you complete lessons 3 and 7 in *Becoming a Church that Cares for the Abused* online training (www.churchcares.com) before making this call. Click on "preview training" to get access to these two lessons.

- » Explain that you want to know more about what roles they can and can't play if a participant were to express the temptation toward self-harm or harming others.
- » Ask them to explain the limitations of their role when someone is contemplating harm to self or others.
- » Ask them to describe how they would want you to respond (who to call and what to do) if a situation necessitating their services arose.
- » Ask them to describe the best and worst practices they've seen from churches or family members trying to involve law enforcement officers with a loved one who is considering self-harm.
- » Ask if they have someone who would be willing to do a Q&A at a pastoral staff meeting or G4 leader debrief.
- » Ask them if there are other questions they wish pastors and religious communities would ask them.
- » Thank them again for their service to your community.

There are other scenarios that qualify as crises, but do not have an immediate report responsibility. Most crises require the voluntary engagement of the person in distress to receive care. A G4 participant may be on a severe drinking binge, on the brink of bankruptcy, experiencing paranoia due to a mental health condition, or have a comparable crisis. If a participant is unwilling, there is little that can be done to force them to seek out the needed care in these scenarios. The best that can be done is to leverage your relational influence to persuade the participant to seek out and engage in the needed care.

STEP TWO: KNOW YOUR CHAIN OF COMMAND

Exercising this relational influence well begins with knowing your G4 chain of command. Often the first person to become aware that a participant is in distress will be their group facilitator. When a participant is experiencing this level of crisis, the facilitator should reach out to their G4 director for additional guidance and support.[2] The G4 director will contact the counseling consultant and then report back to the facilitator with the requisite recommendations.

In response to the three examples above, the type of recommendations that may be received include the following:

- For the participant on a drinking binge, the counseling consultant would know the local rehabilitation facilities—both inpatient and intensive outpatient—and can provide guidance on how G4 leadership and fellow group members can avoid enabling the participant.
- For the participant on the brink of bankruptcy, the counseling consultant would know local attorneys familiar with bankruptcy law and could advise the spouse (if applicable) how to limit their financial exposure if the bankruptcy is being caused by gambling or drug habits.
- For the participant experiencing paranoia, the counselor could provide guidance on indicators of coherence that reveal whether it is possible to engage a profitable conversation with the participant, how to engage when the participant is incoherent, and where to find the best local mental health resources. The counseling consultant would *not* speculate on potential diagnoses causing the paranoia.

Consulting with a counselor allows other leaders and participants to know that your G4 ministry is doing all that can be done wisely. In the absence of consultation like this, people either abandon the individual in distress or do more than is wise to assuage their conscience and believe they have done everything necessary. These responses either divide the group or burn out the leader.

2. If the G4 ministry is small and does not have a director, the group leader should reach out to the designated member of the pastoral staff who fills this role.

STEP THREE: THE G4 DIRECTOR CONSULTS WITH THE COUNSELOR EFFECTIVELY

Often church leaders do not know how to properly consult with a counselor. The result is that the counselor pulls away from the church leader because the misuse of their role begins to result in ethical violations or liability for the counselor.

Instead, effective conversations between your G4 director and the counseling consultant can provide knowledge to help care for people well. We overview elements of those effective conversations here to allow you to "see behind the curtain" and gain a sense of confidence from knowing how these situations should be handled.

First, it should be clear to both the G4 director and the counselor that the conversation is focused on effective, first-aid level ministry engagement with the person in distress, not on creating a comprehensive counseling treatment plan.

Second, the director needs to communicate with the counselor in a way that respects the counselor role. Below are four basic guidelines. The counselor will ask for additional information that would be helpful.

- Don't share names.
- Do share demographic information and relevant history.
- Do share the nature of the disruption the individual is experiencing.
- Do share the relational resources (friends and family) that are available to help.

These introductory remarks might sound like this:

> "We have a 37-year-old male who is on the brink of bankruptcy and his emotional volatility is starting to impair the ability of the group to function. He says he is weeks away from losing everything. While he hasn't mentioned suicide, the frequency with which he is calling other group members and the intensity of his despair has us worried. He has a wife and two children. If they lost their

> house, we think there are church members that would let the family stay with them short-term. But his lack of a financial plan and emotional flailing has us concerned for whether those church members would be taken advantage of. What do we need to look for (red flags), and where should we point him to ensure our church's care is not taken advantage of?"
>
> "We have a 20-year-old female who is starting to have a severe physical response to an eating disorder. Her hair is visibly thinning, and she hasn't had her period in three months. This week she passed out while walking to her college class. She refuses to talk to her parents, saying they will only shame her. The group is getting concerned enough for her physical well-being that it is impeding their ability to focus on their own growth. What would be the next best step for us to point her toward, and how do we help other group members manage their concern for her?"

Third, your questions should focus on the level of engagement the counselor advises you on. You are not asking for diagnoses or a recommended treatment plan. It would be malpractice for the counselor to provide either to a lay-led ministry. You are asking for guidance on helpful, peer-level engagement and the best available professional resources in your community. In most instances, it is wise to ask, "What are the indicators that a situation like this would require a different response than what we've outlined?"

You should compensate the counselor for their time. Some counselors may choose to donate this time to your church. But as your ministry grows and the number of advisements like this increases, you should revisit whether they are willing to continue donating their time. For the quality of care you are able to provide participants and the peace of mind of your leaders (including burnout prevention), this is a wise investment for your church.

Additional guidance on cooperating effectively in situations like these is given to your G4 director and the counseling consultant in chapter 17 of *Mobilizing*.

STEP FOUR: CONTINUE PROVIDING THE TYPE OF CARE G4 IS DESIGNED TO PROVIDE

In the absence of a clear chain of communication and a good consulting relationship, a crisis like this can distract or derail your ministry for weeks or months. You can begin to lose participants and leaders because of the emotional stress it creates.

The cause of this emotional fallout is often people thinking, *If we can't do everything a participant needs, then we have failed as a ministry.* While emotionally compelling, this belief is not true. Imagine someone goes to the dentist, and the dentist notices something wrong their gums that turns out to be cancer. The dentist would refer the patient to an oncologist. The dentist would not despair thinking, *If I can't fix everything in your mouth, I have failed as a dentist.*

So don't get discouraged when someone needs more in-depth care than your ministry provides. It is right and good to empathize with their pain. But it is also right and good to know your limits and to direct participants who need extra care to appropriate outside resources. Just as a dentist would not see it as their failure if their patient failed to follow their recommendation to see an oncologist, so you and your fellow G4 volunteers do not need to see it as your failure if a participant is unwilling to get the additional care you recommend.

You want to create a culture among your leaders and participants that understands our role: At G4, we want to do with excellence the things that a peer support group ministry can do. For the things that are beyond a group ministry, we want to point people in the right direction. We get advisement from the relevant professionals to make sure we know the difference.

With this mentality in place, continue to do what G4 does. You are doing a good thing. Don't let this appendix on responding to the hardest situations distract you from that.

Appendix C

THE TEN COMMANDMENTS OF G4 SELF-CARE FOR SUSTAINABLE LEADERSHIP

These aren't really commandments (that's just a compelling appendix title), but they are strong encouragements. As you embrace the role of being a G4 facilitator, these are things that you need to keep in mind to thrive in this role. As such, these should also be regular topics in debrief.

1. DON'T QUIT READING YOUR BIBLE DEVOTIONALLY.

Early in your time leading a G4 group, you may be tempted to neglect your personal devotion time because you feel overwhelmed by what you are reading to prepare for G4. Later in your time leading G4, as you get to know your group members, you may begin reading the Bible with their needs in mind. As you take time to study the Bible each day, pause, take a deep breath, and remind yourself that this is your time to have your soul nourished by God's Word.

2. DON'T STOP PRAYING CONVERSATIONALLY.

The more needs we are exposed to, the more we can treat our prayer life like a business meeting with God. G4 exposes you to many people you care deeply about who have many needs. It is right and good to pray for them. But you are not just their shepherd. You are also God's child. God wants to hear *from you*, not just *about them*. You need a relational, conversational prayer life. If this is an area you want to grow in, consider reading *A Praying Life* by Paul E. Miller.[1]

3. PARTICIPATE IN YOUR G4 LEADERSHIP COMMUNITY.

G4 is designed so that you don't have to be a lone ranger. But the availability of this community does not have its intended effect unless you participate in it. Take time to get to know your fellow G4 leaders. Ask about their work, family, and interests. Tell them about yours. These are people who know the unique weight and challenges of being a G4 leader. Because of this, friendships in this community provide a uniquely beneficial relational context.

4. ENGAGE THE DEBRIEF FOR ENCOURAGEMENT AND EQUIPPING.

Some nights debrief is designed to facilitate the kind of relationships discussed in the previous point. Some nights debrief is designed to remind you of why you do what you do. Other nights, debrief is designed to equip you for common challenges in group-based counseling that would be points of discouragement if your skills were not refined in these ways. Don't skip or be mindless during debrief. Engage this time for the sustaining influence each evening is intended to provide.

5. PRIORITIZE FINDING A COLEADER.

In a nine-step curriculum, when someone reaches steps 6 or 7, you need to be asking yourself if they could be a quality coleader. You may also know other people in your church who have a similar story to yours and who would enjoy serving alongside you. The sooner you identify a coleader, the more sustainable serving in G4 will be. Make it a matter of prayer, and be intentional about looking for someone to serve alongside you.

---

1. Paul E. Miller, *A Praying Life* (Colorado Springs, CO: NavPress, 2017).

6. MONITOR YOUR SLEEPING AND EATING HABITS.

Our sleeping and eating habits are two of the more accurate, physical measures of how our soul is doing. When our sleep is disrupted or all we want to do is sleep or we have no appetite or we are eating to distract ourselves from our own emotions, our soul is not doing well. Listen to your body. Don't try to be superhuman. Confide in a friend. Talk with your G4 director. Don't just push through until you crash.

7. TALK ABOUT GROUP CONFLICTS AND LIFE CHALLENGES WITH THE G4 DIRECTOR.

Life inside and outside your G4 group will be hard at times. We shouldn't be surprised by this, and we shouldn't be alone with these challenges. Everything is heavier when we carry it alone. Perhaps you remember being stumped as a child by the question, Which is heavier, a ton of rocks or a ton of feathers? The answer is neither. But the correlated question, Which is heavier, a ton of challenge with a friend or a ton of challenge without a friend? does have an answer. Don't carry the load alone.

8. BE PART OF A SMALL GROUP YOU DON'T LEAD.

We recommend you view yourself as a local missionary commissioned to reach and care for a specific group of people. Perhaps that group is people experiencing addiction, trauma, or eating disorders. Regardless of the topic, viewing yourself as a local missionary helps you see the importance of being a part of a small group you don't lead. Missionaries commonly make the error of becoming so busy planting churches that they don't experience the benefits of church in their own life. Don't fall into that trap.

9. KNOW THE DIFFERENCE BETWEEN A "SEASON" AND A LIFESTYLE.

Christians who volunteer in ministries like G4 are notorious for calling everything that is overwhelming a "busy season." Sometimes we do have busy seasons. There is nothing wrong with that. But if we've actually created an unhealthy *lifestyle*, calling it a "busy season" doesn't make it any better. As you consider leading in G4, you will need to ask yourself, *What am I going to do less of to create space to lead in this ministry?* G4 leaders that last are intentional about pruning some activities to create the capacity to be sustainably involved in this ministry.

10. DON'T NEGLECT YOUR MUNDANE PLEASURES.

Make a list of simple things you enjoy: following a sports team, pursuing a hobby, playing music, going to coffee shops, etc. Tell a few friends on your G4 leadership team what these are. Ask them to ask you, "When was the last time you did [blank]?" This will have two advantages: First, it will help you feel known for more than the group you lead. Second, it will remind you to engage the things that bring joy to your life. When, as a result of G4, you spend a disproportionate amount of time entering other people's darkness, you need to be intentional about engaging the things that bring light and life into your world.